Journalism Online

To Heather, Jamie, Rachel and Sophie
and the memory of my parents

Journalism Online

Mike Ward

Focal Press

OXFORD AMSTERDAM BOSTON LONDON NEW YORK PARIS
SAN DIEGO SAN FRANCISCO SINGAPORE SYDNEY TOKYO

Focal Press
An imprint of Elsevier Science
Linacre House, Jordan Hill, Oxford OX2 8DP
225 Wildwood Avenue, Woburn, MA 01801-2041

First published 2002

British Library Cataloguing in Publication Data
Ward, Mike
    Journalism online
    1. Electronic news gathering   2. Electronic newspapers
    3. Journalism – Data processing
    I. Title
    070.4'0285

Library of Congress Cataloguing in Publication Data
Ward, Mike.
    Journalism online/Mike Ward.
    p.cm.
    Includes index.
    1. Electronic journals.   I. Title.
    PN4833.W37
    025.06'704–dc21   2001053150

ISBN 0 240 51610 9

For information on all Focal Press publications
visit our web site at: www.focalpress.com

Composition by Genesis Typesetting, Rochester, Kent
Printed and bound in Great Britain

Contents

Acknowledgements

First I would like to thank Michael Dell for a little Latitude . . . and Beth Howard of Focal Press for a whole lot more. If patience is a virtue, Beth is indeed well blessed. Thanks also to Margaret Denley for her helpful and professional editing of the script; and to Jenny Welham for giving me the original opportunity.

Many colleagues have provided support and assistance along the way. I am indebted to Andrew Edwards for his constant encouragement and perceptive comments; and to Peter Cole and Alan Rawlinson for their helpful readings of draft chapters. My thanks also to Louise Williams for meticulously transcribing the many hours of taped interviews. And a special mention for Andy Dickinson who generously allowed me to use his illustrations and HTML exercises. Andy also made a major contribution to the chapter on design, as he has to much of my thinking on Online Journalism.

I would like to acknowledge the cooperation of the organizations and individuals who have agreed to have illustrations of their web sites included in the book and thank them for their help. My apologies to those who it has not been possible to contact.

I would also like to thank the many people who agreed to be interviewed, including some whose contribution did not make it to the final draft. Their views and opinions were nevertheless influential and helped to inform my thinking on this challenging subject. In particular, I would like to express my gratitude to

Dave Brewer and Bob Eggington for their encouragement and advice as we in the Department worked to establish Online Journalism at Preston. My thanks also to my students for their stimulation and ideas.

Finally, I owe an immeasurable debt to my family who have endured my prolonged absences in both mind and body as I have laboured to complete *Journalism Online*. Many thanks also to my mother-in-law Audrey for providing a peaceful retreat when the going got particularly tough.

But now, it's done.

Mike Ward

1 What is online journalism?

'Online Media may have come of age. But has online journalism?'

Duncan Campbell, investigative journalist[1]

Dot coms, dot bombs, dot rot and roll

Bob Eggington was sitting in a bar with some US online publishers. Talk, as it has a habit of doing, got round to money; in particular, how to make the Web pay. At that time, Bob was the project director of BBC News Online. The journalists wanted to know the BBC's business model for its online news operation.

> I looked at them and said, 'Well here's my business model. We spend a lot of money to collect a lot of data. Then we make it free on the Web, for anybody to consume, and we don't make any money out of it.
>
> At this point they started grinning and said, 'Hey, that's no business model'. I said, 'No, we just get a bunch of money and we spend it.'

Three years later, reality has bitten, hard. The NASDAQ index of technology stocks has been in free-fall with dot com enterprises

[1] Interviewed in *UK Press Gazette*. July 1999.

dropping like flies. The dot rot has truly set in. Eggington reflects:

> I suppose the laugh was on them . . . because what we were doing at the BBC was what they were doing too. The difference is, the public service model is supposed to work that way. The commercial model is not.
>
> That's why there's been this market correction. This had to happen when you had stocks with a capitalization of several hundred million pounds and the annual turn-over of a medium-sized pub.
>
> But none of that is affecting the people who are thinking about how to make journalism work on the Web. In the end, that's not a commercial issue as much as an intellectual challenge.[2]

Eggington's anecdote reflects the setting for this book. But his optimistic postscript lies closer to the heart of the text. Life in the e-conomy has become something of a soap opera – a steady diet of synthetic drama and excitement, complete with predictable denouements, obvious to all, it appears, except the main characters, such as those who invested heavily in the technology stocks.

As a result, the public's reaction to digital media developments has yawed like a drunken sailor from hopeless optimism to excessive gloom and cynicism. In the midst of such instability, it is difficult to plot a steady course; to settle for the solid advance, rather than the 'paradigm shift'.

One minute we are told that mobile Internet technology such as Wireless Application Protocol (Wap) will revolutionize the way we live and do business. The next minute it is decided that Wap has all the qualities of an uncomplimentary word that rhymes with it. Mobile operators are accused of running 'ludicrous adverts (which) have completely over-positioned this new technology and

---

[2] Interview with author, June 2000.

raised user expectations far beyond a level attainable by anyone at the present time'.[3] Influential commentators, such as Jakob Nielsen, deride Wap for its 'miserable usability'.[4] We live in confusing times.

Hard-headed businessmen are not immune to the excitement. At the height of the mobile Internet frenzy, the UK telecommunications group BT paid the British government £4 billion pounds for a licence to use 'third generation' mobile phones at some future date. At least they cannot be accused of not putting their money where their mouth is.

New economic models have been floated. In his excellent collection of 'Web studies', David Gauntlett (2000) expands on Michael Goldhaber's concept of the 'attention economy'. With so much to see on the Web, and so little time to look, attention has become the new gold standard.

> You can't buy attention . . . you can't make (people) interested in what you have to say, unless they actually find the content of what you have to say engaging. So money is less powerful than usual on the Web. But if you can gather a lot of attention, you can then, potentially, translate that into money.

Note the word 'potentially'. As Gauntlett acknowledges, some of the 'money' made in the attention economy is based on stock market valuation. And we have seen what can happen to that. However, he cites others such as Netscape and Vincent Flanders, who have benefited in more tangible ways.

Of course, the problem is that for every Netscape there have been a thousand net losses. Much of this has been the fault of the digital evangelists, some of whom have elevated hyperbole beyond an art form.

As Greg Knauss explains:

> Twice a year or so, like clockwork, a new technology or paradigm sweeps over the face of the Internet, promising to

---

[3] It-director.com quoted in *Dot Journalism*. (www.journalism.co.uk/ezine_plus/ dotjark/story 141.shtml).

[4] www.useit.com

transform not only the medium, but the very fabric of our lives. 'It's revolutionary!' proponents shout. 'It's amazing. It's the next new thing!'

And instead, it turns out to be, well, nothing. Given a few months in the sun, the next new thing inevitable sags and wilts, either disappearing altogether or simply fading into the background of niche usage.[5]

The innocent are swept up in the lemming rush too. Overnight, companies – widget makers the world over – were told that they *had* to have a web presence. Never mind that they knew as much about content creation and design as the average journalist knows about commerce and balance sheets.

The results, on display for all (and that means the whole world) to see can be painful. In a recent survey of UK companies[6], the content management consultancy MediaSurface found that 77% published out-of-date information on the web. Many companies, they concluded, had 'lost control' of their web sites.

But let's stop there. Time to give the barometer a tap. The needle seems to be stuck again on doom and gloom. Is there no middle ground?

One of the problems, of course, is that the 'digital revolution', with all the attendant hype, is a child of its time. The Internet and its applications such as the World Wide Web have not enjoyed the freedom of other, earlier, media. Radio and television were both revolutionary in their day. But they were allowed to experience their growing pains away from the glare of intense expectation on a global scale. They also didn't have to grapple with that most voracious monster, the marketing machinery of late-twentieth-century capitalism.

If people had bought their first television sets in the UK, to watch the coronation of Queen Elizabeth II, expecting to see the ceremony in full colour from fifteen different camera angles, with edited highlights and slow motion replays, they would have queued up to return their sets afterwards and demand their money back.

---

[5] www.theobvious.com

[6] Published in September 2000 and quoted in *Dot Journalism*. (www.journalism.co.uk/ezine_plus/dotjpub/story 166.shtml).

They would also have given television up as a bad job. As it was, most were just amazed, even grateful, to be able to witness something that otherwise would not have been available to them.

We have seen that, after a tentative start, each new medium has become established, with two significant effects. One has been to 'up the ante' and so, eventually, raise expectations. The other has been to improve communication and so people's ability to share expectations, and disappointments. The irony of people using e-mail and newsgroups to complain about the performance of their technology stocks seems lost on many.

In such an environment, it is not surprising that we have the digitally disappointed. The very word 'correction' has implied for some a return to normality, like setting a ship back on to the right course. The many who chafed against, or even ignored, the initial advance of digital technology feel comforted somehow by recent events.

No, the surprise perhaps is that there are still so many who hope for so much. These people know that something, beneath the market froth, has changed for ever. There *has* been a shift, paradigm or otherwise, in the way we communicate and live. The ubiquitous access to digitized information, enjoyed by an increasing percentage of the world's population, is a genie that has escaped from the bottle and has no intention of going back.

When you can publish to the world from your bedroom, you know something has changed. When you can trace a relative in an earthquake zone by posting a message on a bulletin board on the other side of the world, you know something has changed. The question for these people is not 'if', but 'how'. How has it changed, and, how can this new medium be harnessed to best effect?

For the professional, this is a complex question. Journalists in newspapers, radio and television have taken the core journalistic values, knowledge and skills and applied them to their distinctive medium. How to do the same for online, given its range and scope as a medium, is a question still exercising the minds of many.

Equally, the question has validity for the non-professional. The widget makers and the bedroom publishers are playing the same field as the professionals. They too can benefit from learning how to create effective web content. For, as David Gauntlett remarked, it is the provision of engaging content that gets the attention of the web audience; and where you have content creation, you have journalism.

This brings us back to Bob Eggington's postscript – the challenge of making journalism work on the Web. It is a challenge that lies at the heart of this book and is based on defining what online journalism is and how it can be practised best within this new medium. This, perhaps, is the solid middle ground – the way forward.

Trying to look through and beyond the smoke of current battles, this book is based on the following premises.

- Online is a distinctive medium because it is user-driven and multifaceted.
- All elements of the medium should support the offering of the content.
- The application of core journalistic principles and processes should inform all stages of online content creation and presentation, from the original idea to the finished page or site.
- Online journalism is a broad church – embracing content creation across a wide range of types (e.g. news and information) and settings (e.g. commercial as well as news-based).

Bob Eggington sees this as primarily an intellectual challenge. Yet making web journalism work may have commercial potential as well. As yet, there is no viable revenue model for web publishing. One reason for this may be that too many people do it badly.

There is certainly a commercial prize to be won, according to recent research by the Forrester Group.[7] It forecasts that sites offering news, sport, music and games will receive a share of a US$ 27 billion advertising market in 2005, with US$ 13 billion available through syndication, subscriptions and electronic commerce (e-commerce).

[7] www.digitaledge.org/monthly/2001_01/Forrester.HTM

There is, as ever, a Catch 22. Doing anything reasonably well requires resources, not cutbacks. Yet cutbacks are part of the new reality. As part of its research, the Forrester Group interviewed 75 online content companies and found that, by the end of 2000, only 23% were operating profitably; 55% expected to show profitability by the end of 2001; but 67% were planning to cut costs to achieve profitability by 2002.

It's a hard one to call for the professionals. The *Online Journalism Review* (OJR)[8] reported 'panic in the air' at the convention of the Radio–Television News Directors Association (RTNDA) in 2000. Local television news stations in the United States were once thought to have a great web future. Cross-trailing their web sites on air and vice-versa should have been a virtuous circle. Instead, according to the OJR, they now face 'a vicious cycle, as web sites remain unprofitable and stations refuse to commit the resources needed to make them better'.

Once again, the issue is content. In this case, it is a lack of original material and a profusion of repackaged newscasts. Research quoted by the OJR indicated that 96% of web users had heard of local television news web sites. Only 8% visited one or more on a daily basis.

But the genie is out of the bottle. As the OJR noted:

> Only a few years ago, an RTNDA session on the Internet would have drawn a handful of newsroom nerds. At RTNDA 2000, hundreds of news directors packed a cavernous convention hall to hear ABC's Sam Donaldson warn, 'If you are not in it, you are out of luck. And no one in this room wants to be out of luck.'

Some definitions

It is useful next to discuss terminology briefly, before we examine how journalists can harness the online medium most effectively.

[8] http://ojr.usc.edu

The terms 'digital', 'online', 'Internet' and 'World Wide Web' are sometimes used as if they were interchangeable. There is some overlap, but their meanings are not identical. Let's nail down some definitions.

Digital

The digital process breaks down all information – be it data, text, graphics, audio, still pictures or video – into a sequence of numbers (digits), transports it by wire, cable or broadcast frequency to a destination and then re-assembles it back into its original form.

Digitally stored and transmitted information can be quantified as 'bits'. Until it is printed off, it does not have a physical form. Once it is printed, it enters the real world of you and me, Nike trainers and the Millennium Dome – the world of 'atoms'.

It is not this digital concept per se which has instigated the digital revolution. Rather, it is the recent quantum leap in our ability to apply it powerfully. A technological surge has allowed increasingly large amounts and complexities of digital information to be transported anywhere at the speed of light and then be re-assembled – again at a rate that defies comprehension.

The technology has also reduced the hardware needed, such as microprocessors, to a size that allows ubiquitous access to digitized information – in your home, in your car, in your pocket.

Such technology is permeating the fabric of our daily lives. As a result, we have become blasé about the incredible. We become impatient if our PC takes ten seconds to download a picture from the other side of the world. We have come to expect the stupendous.

Of course, in the midst of such digital advance, the world of atoms continues to exist. Even if you could download a pair of jeans from a fibre optic cable, you would still want to wear them. Virtual trousers could have their drawbacks.

Yet the world of atoms is also being transformed, literally bit by bit. The jeans still exist as a physical entity, but the business of making and selling them is also dependent on the communication of information, and that is changing permanently. As you can now buy your jeans on the Web, you do not need a retail outlet (a twentieth-century totem to the world of atoms, if ever there was one). The manufacturer of the jeans can use e-commerce to purchase the raw materials direct from the supplier. Thus, the traditional wholesale distributor may not be needed – another atomic structure under threat.

If this is the impact on the world of atoms, imagine the shock waves in the world of information. The banking and financial services sector is one part of this world and is currently being ravaged by the digital revolution. High Street branches are closing. Online banking is established and expanding. All the old certainties are evaporating.

Journalism is another sector in the information world. Unsurprisingly, it too faces fundamental changes, as will be seen throughout this book. As Nicholas Negroponte (1996) puts it, 'the change from atoms to bits is irrevocable and unstoppable'. And that was said five long years ago.

Online

This is a generic term often used loosely to describe digital information access, retrieval or dissemination.

If you sit at home and access the Internet via your modem and telephone line, you are going 'online'. Similarly, if a newspaper has a web site to complement its published paper editions, this is seen as an 'online' version of the paper.

'Online' is used in the title of this book because it has a conceptual value, referring to the philosophy underlying this form of journalism (e.g. the new thinking on the role of the reader) as well as a descriptive value for which a term such as 'digital journalism' would probably suffice. It covers research and reporting (access and retrieval) as well as publishing (dissemination) and is not restricted to the Web, as is explained below.

Internet

The Internet is not just the World Wide Web. There has been confusion in the past between the Web and the Internet. They are not the same thing. At the risk of oversimplification, the Internet

Figure 1.1: You can buy online . . . .

is the infrastructure that allows computers to talk to each other throughout the world. The Web is the interface that allows people to exchange, data, text, pictures, graphics, audio and video on the Internet.

There are other occupants of the Internet as well as the World Wide Web. The most well known is electronic mail or e-mail. The Web and e-mail are the two online applications that are currently having the most significant impact on journalism and this book will concentrate on them.

Figure 1.2: You can sell online . . . . (These materials have been reproduced with the permission of eBay Inc. Copyright © eBay Inc. all rights reserved.)

Figure 1.3: You can bank online . . . .

World Wide Web

If you have a PC with a modem you can connect it, via a telephone line, to the Internet and then to the Web. Your PC has to be loaded with a browser. This is the software that allows you to navigate the Web and access its contents.

You also have to sign up to an Internet Service Provider (ISP). The ISP hooks you into the system and provides you with an information storage area.

There is more information on the Web than you could possibly ever read or want to read. So one of the first things you must learn is to be selective. Web information is usually kept on web sites. There are now millions of these, built and hosted by a myriad of organizations and individuals, for example:

- news organizations (e.g. newspapers, television companies and news agencies);
- commercial organizations (e.g. manufacturers, retailers and financial services);
- organizations from national and local governments;
- pressure groups – people wanting to change something, be it in the political, social or ecological sphere;

- not-for-profit organizations (e.g. charities and community groups); and
- millions of individuals, who use the Web to tell the world about their obsessions, beliefs and desires.

E-mail

The Internet can be used to write to individuals or groups via e-mail. Most ISPs offer a web access and e-mail service and most web sites have an e-mail facility. But they are in fact two different systems. You can use e-mail without having access to the Web.

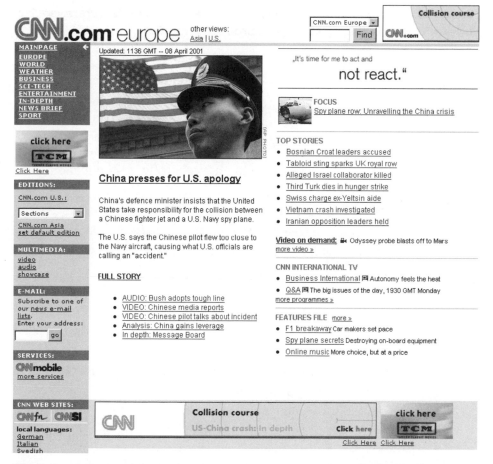

Figure 1.4: The web is now seen as a primary means of communication by many news organizations.

Figure 1.5: Commercial organizations, such as car manufacturers, advise and sell direct online. (Web page reproduced courtesy of Ford.)

E-mail has several distinctive qualities:

- speed – you can type a message and send it very quickly, ranging from the instantaneous to the relatively fast depending on connection times;
- reach – it is global and yet personal; it is not unknown for the big players like Bill Gates to answer their e-mails personally;
- versatility – you can send charts and graphics as well as text by e-mail;
- responsiveness – most people still tend to read their e-mails, despite bulging mailboxes and there is a better chance of a reply because it is so easy to tap out the message then hit the send key;
- flexibility – you can send the same message instantaneously to as many people as you want; and
- accountability – you can set your e-mail up to tell you not only if someone has received the message, but if someone has read it.

E-mail is now everywhere, and not only via the PC and modem. Mobile phones can be used for text messages. Finland is the

Figure 1.6: The Web provides a global platform for 'alternative' voices that might otherwise struggle to be heard.

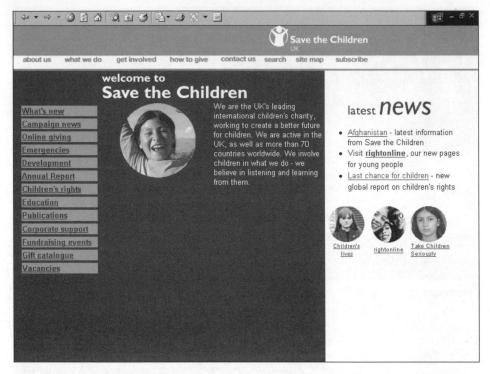

Figure 1.7: The Web gives not-for-profit organizations, such as charities a flexible tool in their continuing campaign for funds and awareness. (Web page reproduced courtesy of Save the Children UK.)

home of Nokia and has one of the highest levels of mobile phone usage per head of population in the world. As Wired journalist Steve Silberman has noted, young Finns use their SMS text messaging system 'as their primary means of mobile communication'.[9]

Silberman's report from the streets of Helsinki gives an intriguing insight into the potential of e-mail:

Like schools of fish, kids navigate on currents of whim – from the Modesty coffee bar to the Forum mall for a slice of pizza or a movie to a spontaneous gathering on a street corner, or to a party, where SMS messages dispatched on the phones

[9] www.wired.com

Figure 1.8: Global = local: Thousands of community sites flourish on the Web, attracting interest from all over the world. (Haslingden Community website is owned by the Rossendale Partnership. It was designed by Pennine Pens and written, edited and maintained by Catlow Communications Ltd.)

summon other kids or send the whole group swimming somewhere else.

American Graffiti for the digital age – same old messages; brand new medium.

Journalism

Chapter 2 is devoted to a full analysis of the key processes and methods which make up journalism, but for now the journalistic process can broadly be described as:

- identifying events, facts, experiences or opinions that may be of interest to your readership;

- acquiring further information and views to develop the initial idea and to verify its accuracy and relevance to your readership;
- selecting from what you have gathered, the material of most value and interest to the readership; and
- ordering and presenting the material with total accuracy and truthfulness and as much style and wit as you can muster in order to inform, stimulate and/or entertain your readership.

This description holds good for journalism within any medium, not just online. However, when you operate this journalism within the online medium, some very interesting things start to happen.

The digital dimension explained earlier has an impact on each of the stages in the journalistic process. It allows both the journalist and reader to do what they did before (e.g. access information), only more extensively and quickly. It also lets them do brand new things. For example, readers can contribute to the storytelling by submitting their own experiences. Just as with banking and financial services, the old certainties start to be challenged.

What makes online journalism distinctive?

So what is so special about online journalism? What does it mean when those two words are put together. Do one and one make three? Is something new and distinctive being created?

The four stages of the journalistic process listed above can crudely be aggregated into two sections. The first is researching and reporting – that is what you 'gather in' as a journalist. The second is story construction and publishing – that is what you 'send out'. Of course, there are cross-overs in this simple division. If you report 'live from the scene', you are sending out information. However, most reporting is used for information and opinion gathering, and that is where it sits in the model used for this book.

The detailed application of online journalism techniques will be explained in subsequent chapters, but it is useful here to outline briefly some of the potentially distinctive qualities of journalism online, when applied to the core journalistic activities of researching and reporting as well as story construction and publishing.

Online researching and reporting

When researching a story, you may have many different sources of information. These can include previous stories, original documents, raw data, press releases or information from individuals.

An increasing amount of this information is being digitized and placed online, bringing with it the potential to transform the journalistic research process. If you know where and how to look, you can benefit from the following:

- the range of access to sources – be they people, documents, data or news archives;
- the amount you can access – millions of documents, stories and contacts;
- the speed of access – if you want to impress the most Jurassic journalist, key a search request into a large database such as Lexis-Nexis. This includes a collection of the editorial content of hundreds of newspapers, magazine articles, company reports, etc, which is updated daily. The speed with which it finds archived articles is wondrous to the most inky-fingered hack. However, what you get back is, of course, dependent on whether you ask the right question in the first place;
- what you can do with the information when you have it (e.g. analysing data on a spreadsheet); and
- the ability to tap into debates, discussions and expertise through e-mail discussion lists or newsgroups – keeping your electronic ear to the ground.

Some of the benefits of online as a research tool derive from being able to do what you could before, only more extensively and quickly. You could probably get much of the information and many of the contacts available online by traditional methods, if you were able to spend about two months on each story.

However, some of the information is brand new. As individuals can publish online, material is entering the public arena that previously would never have seen the light of day. Journalists can also reach out and ask for information.

Such researching power is appreciated by those who were unable to enjoy its benefits, because they conducted their landmark journalism in a pre-digital age. Harold Evans made his name as editor of the *Sunday Times* in the 1970s with campaigning journalism such as the Thalidomide compensation story. Evans acknowledges the value of the Internet for today's journalists. He told the *UK Press Gazette*:

> If we'd had the Web back then and could flash forward to a time when most of the population have computers, we could go on the web and say, 'Anyone who took the drug Thalidomide between these dates, please get in touch with us.' Or instead we'd have an interactive chat line . . . we could (also) have saved a lot of time by researching the scientific data electronically.[10]

The analysis of large amounts of data for trends, discrepancies or other results is a powerful new tool for the online journalist. Why should your readers be interested in data? Data is dull, surely? Well perhaps not if it sheds light on the people who spend your readers' taxes and how well they are doing it or if it exposes the levels of crime in your readers' neighbourhoods and how well the police are coping.

Such data analysis lies at the heart of the Computer Assisted Reporting movement, which is now established in the United States, but has yet to take a hold in other countries such as the UK. There have been fewer impediments to new practice in the other area of journalism – story construction and publication.

Online as a publishing medium

Having gathered and selected their information, journalists want to share it with their readers. That is, after all, what it's all about.

The publication processes of the 'old' media are quite complex. Publishing a high-volume daily newspaper is an intricate business,

---

[10] Interview in *UK Press Gazette*. 3rd March, 2000.

requiring the synchronization of many different activities by a large range of people.

However, as an information dissemination tool, it is still quite crude. Even if the paper runs to several editions, when it is done, it is done and will not be done again for another twenty-four hours. And what you get is what you get. Take it or, as an increasing number in the last decade have done, leave it.

The daily newspaper may have dramatic headlines and dynamite content, but it is not particularly dynamic as an entity. It has a relatively static relationship with its reader. Its daily mission is to find the right formula, to define what are the right 'buttons' for the reader and hit as many as it can in each edition. If it hits enough buttons, the reader will buy it, and that is about it – letters to the editor, reader focus groups and other market research not withstanding.

Publishing online can both open new avenues in information dissemination and build a more dynamic relationship with the reader.

Information dissemination

Immediacy

It used to be said that radio was the most immediate medium. Yet most radio stations only offer you news on the hour or half hour. They put it in boxes. Sometimes it does escape. 'We now interrupt this programme to bring you a newsflash' may be the stuff of B movie fiction but it does happen. However, it is a rarity on stations other than those with a rolling news format. The word 'interrupt' says it all – 'We can only give you one thing at a time so we have to stop one thing (e.g. interview with pop star) to give you another (e.g. newsflash).'

On the Web, there is the potential to update your news, showbiz and any other pages simultaneously and repeatedly, minute by minute, to give both the latest news and low-down on the pop star. A single news site can post dozens of different updates on stories every few minutes. Immediacy supercharged by such flexibility is a potent tool, particularly for breaking news. However, note, again, the word 'potential'.

Multiple pagination

A web site can have hundred of separate pages, linked to each other but also capable of being read and understood in isolation. This increases the amount and range of both the news coverage and the potential audience.

Multimedia

Web sites can offer, with varying degrees of user-friendliness, text, audio, graphics, animated graphics, still pictures and moving pictures. TV is king but video so far has been the Cinderella of web publishing – or perhaps ugly sister would be a better description. Tiny, fuzzy, jumping pictures of what you can see anyway on television (e.g. television news reports) have belied the web's cutting-edge reputation.

The problem is that video contains an awful lot of 'bits' of information and they cannot all travel down the pipe (usually a telephone wire) to the PC quickly enough. The situation is improving. This digital information can be compressed to reduce the amount of space it uses and the size of the pipe (bandwidth) will also increase. Even within current restrictions, the sites of the BBC and CNN (which want to exploit their existing video news resources) are showing what can be done.

Multimedia can provide multiple textures to journalism. For example, you can hear the eye-witness account while reading the journalist's report. Although the application is still rudimentary on many sites, the potential is there and it will be realized, particularly when television and the Web converge.

Flexible delivery platforms

A single online news provider can take one piece of information and put it on a web news page, include it in a searchable database of information or send it to a mobile phone display screen. How to 're-purpose' content to harness this flexibility of online delivery is pre-occupying many news organizations at present. The economics of re-purposing are very attractive. Gathering the information, particularly in news, is often the expensive part. Once you have the information, it makes sense to get it to as many people and in as many ways as possible. It is probably the only thing accountants and journalists agree on.

Archiving

Exploring a well-resourced web site for content is like playing a game of three-dimensional chess. You can sit in the middle of the site and go forward (immediacy), sideways (links to sites, related stories and interactivity) or down into the archive.

Archives are particularly effective for news web sites. As they mature, they build into a useful resource of material which is both archived and, equally importantly, searchable. This can provide an important context to current reportage on the site as well as a research resource in its own right.

The relationship with the reader

Non-linear construction and consumption of content

This is an awful mouthful, but it is very important. So, let's return to the example of radio to explain.

Radio is a linear medium. The audience is fed the content in a line. Interview is followed by presenter, then weather report, traffic news, music, news, etc. When a listener hears a radio news bulletin, he or she cannot say 'I will have item two, five and six, but I don't want the rest.' In reality, listeners will tune in and out mentally, but they have little other control, other than retuning their set to another linear feed (different station) or switching off completely.

The Web is based on non-linear consumption. So, people do not have to go from item one to two to three. When choosing the stories that interest them, they can, and do, go from four to thirty-six to fifteen to two and so on. It is a web, not a line. When a series of carefully selected and presented news items is posted on the Web, bonded together by immediacy and audience relevance (a reasonable description of a news section), it is possible that 50% of the readers will not read 75% of it.

The consumption pattern is driven by the audience, not by the provider. And it is non-linear consumption. This suggests a need to re-think the traditional storytelling process; to deconstruct and reconstruct it for an online audience and their non-linear consumption patterns. If, instead, you continue to present the central events, issues and opinions surrounding a story as a single homogeneous digest, as a newspaper journalist usually would, you will end up with a single block of on-screen text. This may require a lot of scrolling (which people do not like to do). It also limits entry points for the other complementary elements of the online medium, such as multimedia and links to other sites.

You will also have excluded perhaps 50% of your potential readership. When reading a story, people do not want to wade through A, B, C, D and E to get to F, the section that interests them. Indeed, they may not know that F exists. However, if F is offered as a separate story, able to stand alone, but also linked to A, B, C, D, E, G, H, and I, you will attract the F readers. In other words, having gathered the information, if you are able to construct it as a series of related stories which together provide the total coverage, but which could also be read in isolation, you are likely to attract and keep a larger and more varied readership.

Interactivity

This audience-driven consumption is an important element of interactivity. It allows the consumer to interact with the product. However, there are other levels:

- the consumer interacting with the provider, the most obvious example of which are the readers who e-mail journalists with their views on what has been written or to give further information;
- the consumer interacting with the consumer, for example the use of message boards on web sites allows readers to exchange views and information; this can provide different textures and perspective to a story; and
- the consumer can also become the provider – as the online medium matures, some of the voices from 'out there' are becoming more authoritative and confident, making a contribution to the main content.

This final dimension of interactivity can be unsettling for journalists. It challenges the whole premise of the journalist as 'gatekeeper' and information provider. It also raises all sorts of issues about the accuracy, veracity and perspective of that information and reportage. Yet some online journalists are embracing the opportunity.

Out There News, run by ex-Reuters journalists John West and Paul Eedle, is an Internet news agency which welcomes reader involvement. Its coverage of world affairs has attracted e-mail contributions from the informed and knowledgeable, including the people on the ground in areas of conflict.

West told the *Press Gazette*:

> Those people, by their knowledge and experience have a stake in the story. Our ideal would be to produce more stories without any journalists at all. . . . Journalists have to come down off their pedestals because when you do, you discover that your audience knows at least as much about the subject as you do.

Eedle added, 'The "I know all about it, pin back you ears and I will explain" attitude is out.'[11]

Online journalist Steve Yelvington agrees:

> I think journalism in our time has grown up in a sort of lecturing environment. It is 'the journalist sees all, knows all and tells all . . . and the rest of you guys should sit down, shut up and listen'. But what we can have now is a conversation. And, with it, should come the admission that we as journalists do not see all and definitely do not know all.[12]

Linkage

The traditional role of the journalist is further challenged by the online capacity to link readers to other sites. A newspaper could run a story about, for example, lack of funding for school repairs

[11] Interview in *UK Press Gazette*. 23rd July 1999.
[12] Interview with author, June 2000.

in its area. It might contain a news piece and several related features or fact files. The online version of the paper could offer all of that, but also link the reader to the web sites for the local education authority, the relevant government department, the schools' inspectorate, local pressure groups, teachers' unions, the headteachers' association, political parties, etc.

To some reporters, referring the reader to the source must feel like professional suicide, inviting redundancy. Light the blue touch paper and retire immediately; preferably on a decent pension.

However, linkage only changes the journalist's role, it does not destroy it. As Steve Yelvington points out, the journalist is still needed:

> The old model has the editor or reporter as a defence against bad information. 'We only pass that which we deem to be true.' That works when the medium is a primary provider of information. But no medium is a primary provider anymore. We live in a world where information sources now overwhelm us. You can't stop the flow of information. What you can do instead is take the user or reader by the hand and lead them towards the light. I think we as journalists have a function there, to sort through and point out. But more the function of a guide, rather than a gatekeeper. Because the chance to take control . . . that's over with.[13]

What has been the effect of all this on journalism so far?

As we have seen, each one of the distinctive qualities of online can have a fundamental impact. The arrival of this 'fabulous monster', as Brian Appleyard[14] memorably describes the Internet, has told us as much about the world of journalism and how it reacts to change, as it has about the change itself.

Many journalists have struggled to come to terms with going online for research. There is an issue about access. Some newsrooms, particularly in the UK, have been slow to provide the

[13] Interview with author, June 2000.
[14] *New Statesman*, October 1999.

necessary facilities, even the basics such as an Internet connection. However, there are also organizational barriers. It takes time and training to learn how, for example, to make the best use of search engines. In addition, if your news gathering has been built around access to a limited amount of information, how do you come to terms with access to an unlimited amount?

The ability for web pages to run text, graphics, still pictures, video and audio poses further questions. The readership will see this as an opportunity. The journalist may see it as a problem. Learning how to conduct and record a brief audio interview onto mini-disc is not rocket science, but how many sites run by print-based news organizations offer audio? Often there are cultural as well as organizational obstacles to overcome.

Journalists are actually deeply traditional. They become wedded to certain ways and find it hard to change. The newspaper that is published every afternoon has a news production cycle to match. It sets the rhythm of the day. However, if that paper is serious about going online, it will have to raise the tempo. As Howard Kurtz[15] from the *Washington Post* remarked, 'newspapers are transforming themselves into 24-hour news machines . . . the result has altered a tradition-encrusted newsroom environment that has never had to deal with round-the-clock deadlines'. Yet there are still newspaper web sites that state 'This page will be updated every day at 2 pm.' It is a contradiction of the medium. Increasingly, it is also an untenable position in the 'I know what I want and I want it now' news consumer market.

As we shall see, the arrival of online journalism has challenged the primacy of news, the relationship between reporter and reader and the current skills package of the journalist. News and features have given way to 'useful content'. Journalists are told they have become 'information architects', but do not know what that means.

But journalism in the online world is a broad church, encompassing a wide spectrum – from news to information, from investigative journalism to re-purposing content, from multimedia interactions to bullet point lists, from intricate sites to the simple e-zine.

---

[15] *Washington Post*. 7th September 1999.

It can accommodate all of this because, running through it, like a golden thread, is the core journalism – the identification, collection, selection and presentation of information. And that is what we will turn our attention to in Chapter 2.

Further reading and references

Gauntlett, D. (2000). *Web Studies*. Arnold.

Hall, J. (2000). *Online Journalism*. Pluto.

Levinson, P. (1999). *Digital McLuhan*. Routledge.

Negroponte, N. (1996). *Being Digital*. Coronet.

- http:// www.bbc.co.uk – including the flagship news section and details of jobs. It is an impressive resource.
- www.cnn.com – CNN. The one and only. Now presented in three different 'editions', namely the original site plus Europe and Asia.
- http://dailynews.yahoo.com – Yahoo Daily News, consists predominantly of agency wire stories, but this is how many people like their online news.
- www.guardian.co.uk – of the UK newspapers, the *Guardian* has probably tried hardest to produce a distinctive online product, both in style and content.
- www.journalism.co.uk – DotJournalism. A useful UK-based site with news, jobs and the best bit of British virtual real estate.
- www.newmediastudies.com – do not be put off the home page because this is an invaluable resource.
- www.redherring.com – news and information on the business of technology.
- www.telegraph.co.uk – the Electronic Telegraph (the online version of the *Daily Telegraph*) has one of the best archives of the UK-based online newspapers.
- www.salon.com – the online magazine.
- www.slashdot.com – the site with the best tag line on the Net, namely 'news for nerds. Stuff that matters'. A good example of user-driven content.
- www.thestandard.com – news and information on the Internet economy.
- www.wired.com – an essential window on the digital world.

2 The core journalism

'Straight. No chaser.'

Thelonius Monk[1]

'You cannot teach journalism'

Enter any newsroom and talk to a seasoned pro, and he or she will probably tell you that journalism cannot be taught. Yes, young raw talent can be honed and sharpened by working alongside the experienced journalist. But essential qualities such as having a nose for a good story cannot be implanted. They must be there in the first place. You are either born with ink in your veins, or you are not.

Some journalists like to envelop the journalistic process in a certain mystique. The 'journalism cannot be taught' argument is one manifestation of this. It suggests journalism is some higher art form that can only be practised successfully by those blessed with a natural ability. This is not true.

Good journalism at the professional level *is* a skilful, sensitive and imaginative process. It can be exacting and challenging and much harder than it looks. Its exponents deserve more respect than they usually get.

[1] Composition by the jazz pianist Thelonius Monk.

It is true that some individuals have a natural aptitude for important elements of the journalistic process, such as asking complete strangers personal questions or displaying quick witt-edness and lateral thinking on the back of two hours sleep. There are people who are definitely better at journalism than others – better researchers, reporters, designers and, most tellingly, better writers. However, that doesn't mean that the fundamentals, the core journalism, are not within the grasp of many people. There may still be ink, but not as a blue-blooded birthright. The Fourth Estate is not a monarchy; it is a republic. In the online world, it has the potential to include the millions who are researching and publishing on the web each day.

As this chapter will demonstrate, processes such as news identification, collection, selection and presentation can be explained and learned. There is no mystique. Indeed, many of these activities are rooted in concepts of the utmost simplicity. Core journalism can be taught.

The core journalistic process

This statement will be anathema to many journalists, but journalism is a process. It can be articulated as requirements, structure and outcomes. It does not have to be a sterile process, lacking in flair and imagination; but these are not the only ingredients.

At its core, the process has four stages:

- identify and find news and/or information which will attract and interest the key audience/readers;
- collect all the materials needed to tell the story/provide the information;
- select from the collection the best material; and
- present that material as effectively as possible.

Journalists working in print, radio or television follow this sequence to produce stories as a complete package, a digest of events and information that is presented to the reader en bloc and which cannot be unpicked.

Online, as we have seen, can be different. The web is a non-linear medium, within which the readers can choose what they want and leave the rest. Even so, as subsequent chapters will demonstrate, the 'four stages' still apply, both to the construction of most of the *individual components* of content (e.g. news stories, information and audio files) and the arrangement and presentation of the total resource. These four stages are central to the process of journalism online and will form the framework for the rest of this chapter.

Identify and find – what is news?

As this is the starting point, it's not surprising that every textbook on journalism devotes a large section to this vexed question. However, it has an additional importance within the online medium. When the user can both choose their content and publish it, definitions of news become blurred. But criteria are useful because from them you can build guidelines for effective practice. So let's identify the 'traditional' determinants of news and then see where they take us within the context of online.

What is news? When you read a newspaper, watch a television bulletin or visit a news web site, you might reply, 'Well it is obvious. This is news. These are obviously the things they put in newspapers etc.' However, unless the story is so momentous that everyone expects it to be covered, news involves a series of choices. Somebody, somewhere in the news production chain, says, '*This* is what we are going to spend our time bringing to the public's attention and not *that.*' Even the momentous stories involve choices, such as which part of the story will be told and from whose perspective.

The key question is 'What informs these choices?'. This book has no pretensions to be a media theory text. Suffice it to say that there are fundamental influences which impact on journalists, albeit often subconsciously, every hour of every day when they are making these choices.

News values

One factor in the decision making is the individual journalist's set of values and beliefs. Defining news value, despite the best efforts of the most neutral journalist, is a subjective process. It is shaped by the journalist's education, upbringing, location, environment, beliefs and, if they have any, morality.

A second factor is the organizational structure of most newsrooms. News gathering is usually a team effort. To operate effectively, the team needs a shared set of values for defining and measuring newsworthiness. There is constant debate in every newsroom about what is the strongest story of that minute, that hour, that day. However, this debate takes place within the context of agreed criteria. The argument is whether the apple is a Granny Smith or a Golden Delicious. They all *know* it's not a peach.

This encourages a dominant news agenda to emerge, which becomes rigid under the repetitive pressures of daily news gathering. Reflection can give way to automation in the face of the increased demands and reduced resources, which are a feature of modern newsrooms.

David Randall (1999) talks of a journalistic culture within news organizations that extends even beyond dominant news agendas to influence all levels of activity.

> This culture is like a trade secret handed down from master to apprentice – a constantly evolving (or degenerating) received professional wisdom. It sets what editors and their executives regard as a good story or dismiss as 'boring', and determines the subjects they think as 'sexy' and those that are not. It also creates the moral atmosphere of a paper and is thus far more responsible for the ethics that are in daily use on a paper than any theoretical commandments.
>
> This culture determines what is admired in journalists and desired in their work. It has something to do with news value, but is better characterized as 'news instinct'. This can either be a genuine ability to see meaning and interest in what

others might overlook, or, in its degenerate form, the artful technique of presenting the mundane as the unusual.

A third factor in the choice process is the dominant socio-economic system within which the journalist operates. This determines the majority/minority subjects, the majority/minority voices, the majority/minority issues and what gets ignored entirely.

Most media outfits are commercial operations, so they strive to maximize audience and readership. In such a system, the journalists' news agenda will tend to reflect the commercial imperative. They will write for the majority. The web is not immune from this homogenizing process. As online becomes established as a mass medium, it is attracting the major corporations. They are using the power of established media (e.g. magazine advertising and television cross-promotions) to attract new audiences to online. As a result, the tastes and media consumption patterns of these new audiences will probably be more rooted in the traditional media and therefore, they will differ from those audiences who were attracted to the Internet and the web as it developed because it *was so different*. The news agenda of the majority will probably come to the fore again.

This trend is unlikely to be reversed. With every AOL–Time Warner type tie up, the corporate grip will tighten. Syndicated news services will diminish the distinctiveness of major sites. As it is the web, the individual voices will still be there. The minority news agendas will have a forum, but you will have to look a bit harder to find them.

A final factor to be considered when exploring the definition of news value is the quality of the individual journalist. Some journalists are happy to be given a story idea by the news editor, secure their two standard interviews for and against, and then hammer out their word allocation. Such journalists tend to react rather than initiate. They rarely question what they are covering and how they do it because they are comfortable with the existing process and news values. They are, in essence, lazy.

David Randall (1999) argues that there are only two forms of journalism – good and bad. He places creativity, originality and a questioning mind at the heart of good journalism:

> Good journalists challenge the conventional inside their offices as well as outside them. They have ideas, they ask questions of traditional methods and want to try new ones, they say: 'Why don't we do this? Or that?'. They hanker after subjects that newspapers normally do not touch, and new ways of tackling ones that they do. Whenever they hear the phrase 'This is how we always do things', they grow restless. They do not accept the time-honoured divisions between news and features. They hate stories written to a formula. They reject the assumption that certain subjects and ideas are 'beyond' their readers. They believe that good journalism is universal in every sense.

Lazy journalists put news in boxes – categories such as crime, courts, council, sport and 'softer' items such as fashion or music. Such journalists do not reach out to their readers to find out what interests them, to see if these boxes have any relevance to their lives. This approach looks increasingly redundant within the user-driven online medium. Readers can make their own boxes if they want. The online journalist can give these users the raw materials, not just a finished product.

However, there is evidence that some readers still want the daily digest, their news selected and packaged by the journalist. Online can, and does, accommodate both approaches.

Whether you are providing building blocks of information for the user or a finished article, here are some suggestions for maintaining a fresh outlook:

- ask yourself whether you know who you are writing for;
- before you embark on *any* story, ask yourself whether it will engage the reader;
- try to cover new ground (e.g. a new topic area) every week;
- at least once a month, try something experimental both in form

and content (even if it is in your own time and not for publication); and

■ encourage feedback from your readers.

Defining news value

Having issued all the warnings, are there any simple rules for defining news value? Yes, too many. But they revolve around one simple tenet, namely that news is whatever the reader thinks it is. On the face of it, this is not helpful, but it does point the way forward. It shows that, to define news value, you have to identify the triggers that make a reader think something is newsworthy.

Trigger 1 – relevance

The question a journalist must always ask is 'Can the reader relate in any way to my story?'. Relevance is centred on two communities.

■ Geographic communities – these have been the bedrock of much of the journalism in the 'old' media. Local papers, radio and television stations all have their raison d'être rooted in their relevance to a community defined by geography; the idea that people want to know what is going on in their own backyard.
■ Communities of interest – these are based on common interests, concerns, occupations and activities and cross any geographic boundary. Most parents of teenage children, irrespective of their neighbourhood, will relate to stories about drug use among that age group. They will be bonded by a common interest and concern.

The lines between geographic communities and communities of interest can be blurred. One can morph into the other. Major league sports teams were once firmly rooted in their geographic community, bastions of local identity and expression. Many are now marketed globally. They have become brands. The English football club Manchester United probably has more fans world-wide than the entire population of its geographical base, the city of Manchester. Supporters in Singapore and Sydney may never meet on the terraces of the club's ground Old Trafford, but they share a common bond and kinship. The fans of Manchester United have become a strong community of interest. Their only geographic community is global, served of course by e-mail, web sites and all things online.

The accepted wisdom is that late-twentieth-century living and the Internet have encouraged communities of interest at the expense of geographic communities, particularly in cities. No-one knows who lives next door, but they can tell you everyone in a ten-mile radius who is interested in windsurfing because they have met through newsgroups, set up their own club web site, etc.

Here we find ourselves in 'paradigm shift' country again. This trend towards communities of interest, at the expense of geographical communities is evident, but it almost certainly has been exaggerated and generalized. Nevertheless, it has caused introspection and, on occasions, a crisis of confidence among the 'old' media, such as the local newspapers who have questioned their traditional role of serving the geographical community. Television has followed the trend with a deluge of 'lifestyle' programming, with the focus clearly on communities of interest.

Some charge the 'new' media with encouraging this development. If so, it also has the technology to arrest it and there are those who are using it. Web sites can now deliver local news to online users as defined by their post (zip) code. This is clearly a definition of readership by geography. Mobile phones can identify the precise location of callers and deliver information that is immediately relevant to their needs, such as directions to nearby amenities.

There is, it seems, still a future for geographic communities when defining news and information value and relevance for the online audience.

Trigger 2 – revelation

Readers may also consider a piece newsworthy if it is telling them something new or at least something they did not previously know. On the web, this is as likely to be information as straight news. Whatever it is, the motivation for the readers is the same. They want to fill gaps in their knowledge.

Trigger 3 – arousal

Unique, dramatic or entertaining news will arouse reader interest more than the mundane. This is the most elusive trigger and the one journalists most frequently try too hard to find. Perfectly good stories can be ruined by a pumped-up presentation – spoken or written. Adjectives abound. The aim is to give the story added value, but the result is usually is the opposite. None of this diminishes the news value of arousal, if it is the genuine article. These criteria can be overlaid with an additional characteristic to enhance and broaden news value – human interest. People like to read about people. Facts and figures or abstract concepts are rarely as attractive.

This interest is not just manifested in the 'kiss and tell' stories of the tabloid press. Politics, economics and social issues are also personalized by journalists who often portray complex issues through the eyes and actions of individuals.

The human interest tradition is by-passed by some users of the web who will specifically seek information and a non-personalized treatment of politics, etc. However, as noted earlier, online is not a 'zero-sum' game. There is room for both approaches. The reader chooses.

The agents of news

So much for the adjectives that describe news triggers – unique, new, relevant. But a unique what? A new what? A relevant what? What are the vessels to hold these emotions and reactions? What are the agents of news?

The *Concise Oxford Dictionary* defines 'news' as 'tidings, new or interesting information, fresh events reported'. If you change the order, you are close to the three main agents of news – information, actions and quotes.

Information

Distinctions between news and information can be blurred at the best of times. On the web, as we have noted, they often merge into one. A Jimi Hendrix web site may contain an archive giving details of previous recordings with links to other sites. The

Figure 2.1: On the Web, where does news end and valued information begin? This site provides a platform to sell Hendrix's music but for his many fans it can also be a source of information they can't get elsewhere – the news that matters to them.

information there is neither news according to the traditional meaning or new in the topical sense. Nor is it intrinsically dramatic or unique.

Yet who is to say that a Jimi Hendrix fan, a member of that particularly loyal community of interest, might not find information there about an obscure recording that is new to him or her – a revelation in fact. That fan would probably regard it as the most important piece of both information and news he or she had read all day.

That is why this author believes journalism online must be a broad church. There is no place for a false hierarchy between news and information imposed by the journalist when it is the user who defines what is news to him or her.

As Nora Paul, Director of the Institute for New Media Studies at the University of Minnesota, explains:

> Media companies need to think of themselves as information providers. Information is more than just the current events on any particular day. It is also the information that helps people make decisions in their lives and make choices. Hopefully the media tradition of giving objective and accurate information, but now about how people can live their lives, will play into all kinds of content.[2]

Actions

'Give us a minute and we'll give you the world' is the famous war cry of the radio news bulletin. 'We'll tell you *what's happening* around the world.' The actions of individuals and armies have shaped our history, and journalism, as we are constantly told, is the first draft of history. Action makes news.

Quotes

What people say can be as newsworthy as what they do. However, it usually depends on who they are. The utterances of unknown individuals seldom make headlines. What is said only becomes newsworthy in relation to who is saying it.

[2] Interview with author, June 2000.

Get the right combination of person and quote, and you've got news – at least, that's what politicians try to persuade journalists every day.

Original and existing news

The next important fundamental to understand about identifying and finding news is that a lot of it isn't new at all.

Most journalists spend a large part of each day working with what is already known, trying to find a development. The aim is to take an existing story a stage further, to reveal additional information, action or quotes, which will be of relevance to the readership. The development may be new, but much of the rest of the story will be 'background' or, to put it more crudely, a re-hash of what has been written before. This is known as the development of 'existing' news. It is the staple activity of much news journalism.

There is a certain amount of selfish posturing by some journalists about the development of existing news. For them, it smacks of recycling – worthy but dull. This is putting the interests of the journalist before the needs of the readership and audience. People want to know about developments in stories they have been following, because the story interests them. It would be a disservice not to tell them. Equally, if taken to excess, developing existing news can become introspective and again exclude the reader. The pursuit of a development in a story can become more important to the journalist than the development itself or may be easier than looking for something fresh.

Some news *is* brand new. Crime and accidents are obvious examples, but there are many others. The coach of a football team is sacked, a politician exposed, a rock band splits up. These events each fit within the context of the lives of the football team, the political party or the band. Yet the news event is sufficiently different or unexpected to be seen as something new – the starting point of a story that itself becomes existing news and, so, ripe for further development.

This 'brand new' material can be classified as 'original' news. It often has more impact than developments of existing news. It can be more dramatic, or revelatory. However, it is also a scarcer commodity. The best news teams try to get a good balance of both original news and developments of existing stories in their coverage.

The life-cycle of news

Concepts of original and existing news do suggest that there is a temporal continuum for news and, in a sense, this is true. One can see it as the life-cycle of a news story. It has the following four stages. However, because news is a unique animal, not every story goes through each stage of the life-cycle.

Stage 1 – preview
Some news, such as the staging of important political summits or major sporting events, can be previewed. News stories announcing they are to take place will be followed by speculation, leaks and further details, all before the events actually happen.

Stage 2 – news event or activity
This is a pivotal point in the life-cycle, when the main news event or activity itself takes place. In the case of breaking 'original' news, such as a crime incident, the life-cycle would start here.

Stage 3 – reaction and further development
So much development of existing news is based on getting people's reactions to the news event – those newsworthy quotes. There can also be further developments in the facts of the story itself. This process of development and reaction can carry on for some time, getting reaction to the reaction to the development, etc. That's when it's in danger of becoming convoluted and boring for the reader. Know when to stop.

Stage 4 – anniversary
Just when you thought it was all over, the human need for a chronology to measure the passing of our lives demands that a story is revisited one year, ten years, fifty years or one hundred years after the original news event.

Sources of news

So much for what is news. But where does it come from? What are
the sources of news? They are many and various, but include the
following.

- Eyes and ears – journalists must be both observant and
  curious. They should find it impossible to walk past a hole in the
  road without looking to see what is in it. They can also rely on the
  eyes and ears of others to provide tip-offs to potential news.
- Individual sources – these are the people who know what the
  journalist wants to know. They have information, expertise and
  opinions and can be quoted. They should not be confused with
  contacts. Contacts can tip off journalists, point them in the right
  direction, give them background or put them in touch with
  sources. Contacts and sources should be logged meticulously
  in a contacts book which should be updated on a daily basis.
- Press releases – they should be approached with extreme
  caution, but not complete cynicism. Just because someone
  wants you to publish something does not automatically mean it
  is not worth publishing. Of course, the information or view
  offered in any press release should be checked, challenged, if
  appropriate, and only given space if the end result is of value or
  interest to your readers.
- Other media – journalists are professional magpies. They will
  scour competing media for ideas, nuggets of information, even
  complete stories, which they can investigate further. 'Other
  media' is probably the biggest source of existing news for
  journalists to develop, which is okay as long as if it doesn't
  become their *only* source of news.
- Newsroom diary – all newsrooms, indeed all journalists, should
  keep an up-to-date news diary. This will list forthcoming events,
  follow-ups, anniversaries, etc. Diary items can also be
  previewed.

The Internet has multiplied the potential sources of news and
information exponentially. 'Other media' can now include newspapers and radio stations from around the globe. 'Press releases'
have been supplemented by whole sites run by governments,

companies, charities, pressure groups, etc., pumping out their particular view on the world.

It is a valuable resource, but should be handled with care. Journalists in the 'old' media are always told to double-source their information – to check and cross-check. Those rules do not change because the information is offered online. If anything, they should be imposed even more stringently because it is more difficult to establish the provenance of material on the Internet.

Identify and find – what a journalist should and should not do

Start with good material

Listen carefully in any newsroom and you may detect the unedifying sound of dead horses being flogged. Research and reporting can be a time-consuming and energy-sapping business. Why do journalists waste these scarce resources on material of little promise, for example stories that:

- have little interest to their readership;
- have been told before; or
- show little development potential?

Of course, to avoid such material you need to know what your readers know and like. Aspiring young journalists sometimes lack the necessary broader perspective, possibly because they are the products of an age of niche marketing and personalized information. They take all they can get on their favourite subject, but leave the rest. As a result, they may know little about nine-tenths of what is going on around them. However, there is a very good chance that their readers will be sitting in the nine-tenths sector. What hope has a teenager of reaching a person aged forty if he or she knows every scrap of minutiae about a film star or sports personality, but thinks the NASDAQ is a rock band from Seattle?

Of course, the web is one of the prime providers of such personalized information, but the best web journalists are those with a broader view. They consume other media. They even read books.

It helps them to raise their sights, place their work in context and introduce their readers to the serendipity factor – in other words, to encourage them to venture beyond the 'Daily Me' to find something on the site and elsewhere that they did not know they would like, something *new*. This isn't subverting people's ability to choose what they want on the web. It's supplementing it. However, to do it, the journalist needs a wider horizon than many of his or her readers.

It is easy to overstate the problem. Some young journalists do the sort of work where their knowledge and love of the minutiae of contemporary culture serves them very well. Others have that broader perspective and even understand the value of history as an essential context. But too many do not. So they gravitate towards stories of little interest to their usually older readership. When they do cover the areas their readers want, they frequently do not know either what has happened or been said in previous coverage. They also waste a lot of time stumbling blindly around the structures that bind the apparently alien worlds of, for example, local politics, financial services or health authorities.

Know your structures

These worlds, and all others, operate within a series of interlinked structures and systems. Local politics, for example, has a structure of elected representatives working with local government officials. It has another structure dividing the authorities between very local, local and regional. Yet another structure divides the work of the authority into different departments and another provides a system of committees of elected representatives for each department. It has a party political system for the elected representatives and an electoral system that defines the constituency for each elected representative, when they will be elected and by which electoral method. On one level, we inhabit a world of structures and systems.

Unless you are a specialist correspondent, you do not have to know everything about a particular field such as local politics. However, you should have a working knowledge of the key structures and systems. Journalists, it is said, have to know a little about a lot. If you do not, you will not only waste large amounts of time fumbling your way through any story, but you will also miss stories because you will not understand their significance within the context of the structures of that particular organization.

Knowledge of such structures and systems can take you quickly and simply to authoritative sources for further information and interviews. Without it, you look and behave like a rank amateur.

Talk of structures and systems is anathema to some journalists. It smacks of 'journalism by numbers' – a joyless world where personal contacts, panache and rat-like cunning are replaced by procedure, spokespeople and bureaucracy. This is a fallacy.

Knowing structures and being able to think laterally are not mutually exclusive. In fact, they are mutually dependent. If you want to keep off the beaten path, it helps to know where the beaten path *is*.

It is also a fallacy that structures only inhabit the mainstream. Every culture and organization has some form of loose structure, the inter-relationship of its key constituents and components. Before daring to venture into a piece about dance music, the 40-year-old reporter had better understand the relationship, if any, between hip hop, jungle, house music and rap, if he or she wishes to retain a shred of credibility with any younger readers. Equally, a knowledge of balance sheets and stock markets is now helpful for sports reporters, given the rapid development of sport into one of the biggest businesses. Everywhere you look, you see structures and systems. You ignore them at your peril.

The representative view

As has been seen, understanding structures can lead you quickly and simply to authoritative sources. But what are these sources and why are they important?

Extrapolation is a favourite pastime of journalism students on their first assignments. They often interview two or three students (usually their flatmates) on an issue such as the standard of university accommodation and then write a piece that starts 'Students are up in arms about . . .'. They paint a picture of students across a campus, united in a common cause. Never mind

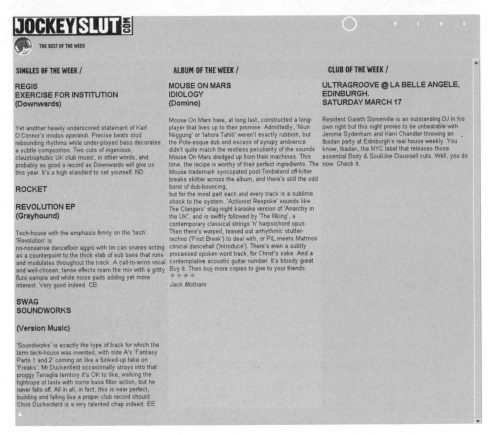

Figure 2.2: Read the text: 'Ibadan', 'post-Timbaland', 'Pole-esque' – structures, structures, everywhere, even in the world of dance.

that they have not spoken to the other 15,997 students to gauge their opinion.

Of course, they cannot speak to all the other students. So what can they do? The simplest approach is to learn about the structure of student unions and councils and how they relate to a university over issues such as accommodation. Then they can interview someone with an overview, such as a student who has been nominated or elected to take up accommodation issues. They should also interview someone from the university to get his or her response.

This approach has two immediate benefits. First the student representative can tell the journalist if other students have complained and if the university has responded. This helps the journalist to establish the scale of the problem, and gauge whether a story should be written at all. Second, the student representative can be quoted as an authoritative source because of their knowledge and elected position. Without this, unless the complaint is dramatic or unique, you will get the dreaded 'so what' response from your readers. Two students are up in arms about their accommodation – so what?

This does not mean that the individual view has no place in any story. Journalism that relied solely on the representative view would be bland and colourless. People want to read and hear about people. They want the eye-witness and personal account. It is the human condition. Effective journalism humanizes stories whenever appropriate and possible.

The individual view can be used most effectively if it is demonstrably representative of a wider concern. You need both perspectives. It is a little like a bottle of lemonade. The liquid is the representative view, the individual accounts are the fizz. If you put your nose in the fizz, but don't drink the liquid, it is unsatisfying, insubstantial and irritatingly ticklish. If you drink a liquid that is lacking fizz . . . well, we all know what flat lemonade tastes like.

Be confident

Journalists must begin with the belief that they will get the story, i.e. with confidence in their own abilities. This does not mean that only screaming extroverts will become successful journalists. Most editors like a balanced ticket on their news team – some who will stick their foot in the door, but others who are more reflective. The latter are less prone to a common affliction among reporters – the knee-jerk association (see the next section). However, even the quiet types need the determination and the self-confidence to be able to pick up the phone and ask someone awkward questions. Journalists must feel able to challenge any viewpoint. To do so successfully, they must be well briefed and confident.

Keep an open mind

'Assume' should be a banned word in all newsrooms. Assuming what the reader wants, assuming the best angle of your story, assuming who is the best contact, assuming what the contact will say when you speak to him or her, assuming what they say isn't newsworthy if it's not what you expected, assuming you know enough or assuming you are right.

Students of journalism often find news development quite testing. They have difficulty getting the balance right between investigating an area of potential news development and having the story cut and dried and half written in their head before they have even spoken to anyone.

They may single out a certain interviewee and approach him or her with a fixed idea of the response they would like. They then assume that somehow the 'story' has fallen down if the interviewee does not give the 'right' answers, even though an analysis of what the interviewee has said might reveal an unexpected, but better, angle. Alternatively, there could be other people to interview.

Similarly, something *not* happening can be just as newsworthy as something that is happening, for example when a local council, police force, hospital trust or government body takes no action following a series of complaints from the public.

It is far better for the journalist to keep an open mind, seeking new angles, perspectives and developments. The most important word in the journalist's vocabulary is 'why?'. Yet it can be the least used.

Get organized

Here lies one of the many paradoxes within journalism. The more disciplined and structured your approach to research and reporting, the more freedom you can enjoy to be imaginative, effective and incisive.

The journalist with the up-to-date contacts book or tidy desk doesn't waste any time when looking for sources of information, so they spend more time using them. The journalist who takes the trouble to find out how the city council or fire authority works will get to the right people earlier and quicker when chasing a story than the one who muddles through. The journalist who prepares thoroughly for an interview with a local politician is more likely to ask the tough questions than the one who thinks it's more productive to let the creative juices flow and wing it.

Collect – conducting interviews

Having identified a potential news story and found the best sources, you have to collect the information you need.

The use of online tools has brought great advances in this area. Gone are the dusty, dog-eared and incomplete cuttings files. As Chapter 3 will demonstrate, the journalist now has access to unparalleled amounts of information. The trick is finding the right stuff.

A reminder here: cuttings files have always been a great way of perpetuating myths and mistakes. An inaccuracy in an original cutting can resurface in later examples and then, with repetition over time, develop a patina of truth. This is an even greater problem on the Web, where material is more difficult to source and yet can be presented immaculately.

In such circumstances, there is no substitute for the other critical element of the news collection process, that is talking to real people. Online journalists must not become over-reliant on data, documents, e-mail and newsgroups. They must also learn the skill of interviewing.

This may seem unnecessary for many journalists who sadly never set foot outside their online newsroom. However, interviewing should not be the preserve of the reporter on the road. It is an essential tool for all journalists. Even those who spend their time 're-purposing' content (e.g. taking stories from one medium and reworking them for online) will need at times to check out elements of the story. They may receive e-mails from readers who have extra information or eye-witness accounts, and these people need to be interviewed.

Interviews can take the following forms and they all have applications for online.

- The research interview – this is aimed at getting background information and fact checking. Research interviews can also be a preliminary to the other forms of interview.

■ The text-based interview – this is getting information and quotes for reproduction in text form, previously newspapers and magazines but now also web sites. The information can extend to descriptions of the interviewees and the interview process itself (e.g. location).

■ The broadcast interview – here the actual interview will be offered to the audience in an edited form. So performance and technical quality are considerations as well as information gathering. Increased use of multimedia will make the broadcast interview a valuable element of online storytelling.

Interviewing is a pivotal activity within journalism. Get it wrong and the mistake will run like a fault line through the rest of your news gathering and be evident in the final story. Stories often suffer because the journalist has gathered too little information, too much information, inaccurate information, the wrong impression or the least newsworthy angle. The root of many of these problems can be traced to poor interview technique.

Why then do many aspiring journalists give both the interview process and their own technique so little thought? Possibly because, compared to recording, editing or page design, for example, talking to someone can seem the most natural thing in the world to do.

Journalists who are accomplished interviewers *can* make it seem like the most natural thing in the world. But that impression belies the hours of preparation they may have undertaken as well as their radar-like listening skills and quickness of thought, acquired through years of experience – all lurking beneath that laid-back exterior.

The importance of preparation

One of the keys to conducting effective interviews is to prepare thoroughly. There are very few occasions when you cannot prepare for an interview. Even if you 'door step' a politician as he or she leaves a meeting, you can prepare beforehand by finding out about the politician, the nature of the meeting and the main political issue of the day. This preparation can take two forms – the specific and the general. The 'specific' is the research focused directly on what the politician's meeting is about. The 'general' is your knowledge of current affairs, including any background to the politician's meeting. The latter is often a lifeline – hence, the old adage that the journalist should know a little about a lot.

This general research should be effortless for journalists. Their interest in information, communication and what is going on in the world should ensure that they are fully briefed on current affairs. Sadly, this is often not the case.

Plan an interview structure

As you research, a possible structure and direction for the interview will begin to emerge. Do not fight this inclination. It is not cramping your style. It will enhance it.

Start by identifying key areas for the interview. Then boil these down to key points. Print them on a piece of paper as bullet points. Never write down your questions verbatim in a numbered list. If you do, you will spend the interview with your head buried in your notepad, reading instead of writing and listening. You will also become inflexible, asking a question simply because it is the next one on your list, even though it may have been unexpectedly dealt with by a previous answer.

You should aim to establish a relationship with your interviewee. That may be as an equal, confidante, counsellor or even confessor. In face-to-face interviews, this requires firm eye contact and positive body language. You can do neither if you are pre-occupied, trying to read your next question and wondering if it is still appropriate.

If you put your key points down as bullets, in large type, with spaces between them, you can read them at a glance, keep track of the content and direction of the interview but also be free to depart this loose 'script' at a moment's notice. Indeed, you may want to do that, if you are exercising the most important of your senses for successful interviews – if you are listening.

Listening skills

Nervous student journalists understandably focus much of their attention on what *they* are saying when they do their first interviews. 'Have I got any killer questions? Are they concise enough? Do I sound authoritative?' Broadcast students also worry about whether they sound sufficiently cool and articulate.

Although these considerations are important, they are less than half the story. You must also *listen* very carefully to all the answers, otherwise your questions will be based only on your prior research and even the most thorough research will not tell you everything. The interviewee, perhaps under the pressure of being interviewed, may reveal something new or say something surprising or outrageous. You will not catch it, if you are not listening. If you do catch it, be prepared to leave your bullet point list to question further and challenge, if appropriate. You can always return to your list for the final questions.

This may seem absurd. Of course, journalists listen to interviewees. Well, not always. And when they do, do they listen closely enough? The inexperienced can be so nervous about the interview and grateful to have got it, they ask their first question and then stop listening. Instead, they fill their heads with their own thoughts. 'How did that question sound? I hope it goes all right. Can I get this all down? I wish my shorthand was better. Is the camera getting this?'

They must train their mind to do three things at once – to concentrate on getting the notes down, to check the bullet points and to listen. If the interview is taped, there is even less excuse for not listening carefully. This mental training may sound easier to suggest than put into practice. But you do it every day. You are doing it now, reading this sentence and wondering when I am going to stop going on about interviews.

Ask a stupid question

Interviews are partly about gathering information, but they also involve a personal dynamic between the journalist and the interviewee. Who is in control? Who is directing the process? Who has the 'upper hand'?

Aspiring journalists need to find a balance, avoiding both incompetence and over-confidence. It's important not to demonstrate fear. However, nor should they try to blind their interviewee with their brilliance and knowledge. Often a slightly diffident approach, underpinned with a thorough understanding, can work wonders. "This might seem like a stupid question . . .' should be the preamble to your most incisive enquiry. It's known as the 'Columbo' school of questioning perfected by Peter Falk in the 1970s TV police series. Each week he would interview suspects, feigning ignorance to gain knowledge. Young journalists sometimes invert this process, with the inevitable disastrous consequences.

Observational and empathetic technique

Feature writers for newspapers, in particular, will employ a range of interview techniques that go beyond the core tasks of gathering news, information and views. These techniques can be applied in other media, including online.

Feature writers often place much emphasis on exploring the character and circumstance of the interviewee, namely who are they and what makes them tick. So as well as concentrating on what they say and hear, these journalists also rely on what they *see*. Such observational reporting also complements a narrative writing style.

Feature writers often choose to interview someone at home or in the workplace because these surroundings will tell them much about the person and help them paint a more vivid picture. Photographs, mementoes, even books in a room, can all reveal new insights and spark off fresh lines of questioning.

They will also take time to build up a rapport with the interviewee. They will check details, demonstrate their desire to get a true picture and even share experiences. This can make it easier to ask the interviewee to relive events and explore emotions without having to employ that most crass of questions, when used in isolation, of 'How do you feel?'.

This technique is not like the hurried news interview. It needs to be face-to-face and usually takes time. Journalists should always act with sensitivity, sincerity and integrity; but these qualities are in particular demand in these interviews. The journalist is asking the interview subject to provide the raw material for a story that will focus on the universal reference points of hope, fear, anger, love and loss, and so engage that largest of all communities of interest – you, me and the rest of the human race.

The best journalists do not put straight reporting and observational technique in separate boxes, only to be taken out when necessary. Both remain 'full on' during any interview and in any medium. Interestingly, television can be less observational than newspaper feature writing, partly because television is a such a literal medium. Newspaper feature writers can interpret their observations and interweave them with their own thoughts, quotes from the interviewee and background research. All are given the same status within that most flexible of mediums – the written word.

The core journalism is not medium specific. It can be applied across the board. However, there are additional skills, beyond the core, that are required to collect news effectively as an online journalist.

Broadcast interviews

Online is a multi media format. You can use text, graphics and pictures, but also audio and video. Technical barriers, such as bandwidth restrictions, currently limit the use of video. These will be removed in time, but they will leave other man-made obstacles that may be harder to dismantle.

Many current online news providers are newspaper organizations. Their journalists are not comfortable working with audio or video, particularly originating it. They've never done it before. There is a cultural barrier. Some may just fear the unknown.

Broadcast interviews are different to text-based interviews, but that does not mean that they are more difficult. It is just a question of modifying technique. All of the core requirements such as preparation, confidence and listening still apply. But there are additional demands.

Audio

The most obvious difference with audio is that the audience actually gets to hear the words exchanged between the journalist and the interviewee. So one of the time-honoured techniques of the newspaper journalist – the leading question – has to be discarded.

If a newspaper journalist asks Mr X, 'Would you say the Mayor has acted far beyond his powers?' and receives the answer 'Yes', the journalist will then report, using indirect speech, that Mr X says the Mayor had acted far beyond his powers. This is no good for an audio interview. The leading nature of the question becomes transparent. Also 'Yes' does not make a sparkling soundbite. Interviewees must express their views in their own words. Getting them to talk is important, but so is getting them to stop. And getting them to say something worthwhile.

As a rule, people do not like having a microphone thrust in their face. It makes them nervous and they become either tongue-tied or they talk too much. Either situation requires the journalist to take as much control of the interview as possible.

But how to get that control? You cannot, and should not, attempt to make your interviewee say exactly what you want. However, you should ensure that the interview has structure, focus and flow. That way, the interviewee will have to address the key points but should also have the freedom to say something spontaneous, maybe even unexpected. You must also get a recording of reasonable technical quality, but this is not rocket science.

The ground rules for conducting interviews offered earlier in this chapter, in particular the need for preparation, are vital to the success of audio interviews. But here are some additional guidelines.

1 It seems obvious, but remember that people will be *listening* to the end product. So make sure your topic is suited to an audio interview. Very technical subjects, laden with factual information, do not usually make easy listening. Also choose an interviewee who is a good talker – someone who is fluent and a clear speaker.
2 Be realistic about how much you can cover. Unless you have a major interview or a very complex subject, limit yourself to key points. This will provide your outline structure.

3 Give some thought to the sequence of questions, so there is a logical flow and order to the interview. Chronologies work best in event-based stories, such as crime or emergency incidents. Issue-based stories need more careful construction so that you can take the listener with you. Do not be afraid to give the interviewee a broad outline of the ground you wish to cover before the interview. The experienced will already know what to expect but it can relax the inexperienced interviewee and result in a better interview.

4 Do your research before the interview, not during it. Questions that gather basic factual information will bore the listener. Use the factual information gathered prior to the recording to pose sharp and focused questions during it.

5 Questions must be open (e.g. 'how', 'why' and 'what' questions, which cannot be answered with a simple 'yes' or 'no'), but not too open. 'Tell me a little about . . .' is a disastrous opener to a question. You are not providing any structure or focus. The interviewee will either tell you too much, or take you at your word and only utter half a sentence.

6 Keep your questions succinct and clear, certainly no longer than the answers! Do not ask two questions in one. It confuses the inexperienced interviewee and lets the others off the hook.

7 Listen very carefully to the answers and be prepared to challenge or put the other side of the argument when appropriate. Try not to interrupt too often. Even the most experienced interviewees must pause for breath, which can give you a chance to get your challenging question in.

8 Use plenty of eye contact. If your interviewee is nervous while he or she is talking, do not make encouraging 'hmms' or repeat the phrase 'I see'. They distract the listener and are a nightmare to edit. Just nod your head and smile, if appropriate.

9 Hold the microphone about nine inches away from the interviewee's mouth and check the recording level before the interview. Be prepared to adjust the microphone position during the interview if the interviewee starts to talk more loudly or quietly. If you get too close to the interviewee, the

recording could distort (digital recorders are particularly unforgiving of such 'overmodding'). If you are too far away, they will sound off microphone ('off mic'), as if they were on the other side of the room. Practice will perfect basic microphone technique.

10 Choose interview locations without intrusive or intermittent background noise. The intrusive will drown out your interview. The intermittent will make editing difficult (the background noise, such as a truck passing, may suddenly disappear as part of the edit, which sounds both unnatural and distracting).

11 If interviewing in a room, take all telephones off the hook and put a 'Do Not Disturb' sign on the door. Avoid areas with hard surfaces such as wooden desktops, glass doors or windows, which offer unsympathetic acoustics. The recorded voices reverberate around the room and can result in poor, booming sound quality.

Pictures

Pictures are a key element of storytelling. We all know the current exchange rate – supposedly 1000 words minimum.

Taking pictures is easy. Taking good pictures is another matter. An indepth account of focal length, depth of field, aperture settings, shutter speed, etc. requires more space than this book allows, so we will concentrate instead on how to avoid taking truly awful pictures. If you are the content provider for a small to medium-sized organization, you may have to include Chief Photographer among your roles. You need pictures that are worth posting on your page.

Your two main components are usually your subject and what surrounds it. Much of the dynamic and structure within a photograph comes from the relationship between the two – both spatial and informative. Remember, however, that the subject is just that and must be the main element of your picture. Too often people do not work close enough to their subject.

- Spatial – this refers to the size and positioning of your subject. Too close and it squeezes out the surrounding context, too far away and it can be dominated by the surroundings. If you position the subject off-centre, it can add perspective.

■ Informative – surroundings that are inconsistent or even contradictory to the subject weaken the message. For example, you would not take a picture of protestors seeking safer speed limits in their neighbourhood and show them standing by an empty road. However, if your background is unnecessarily busy, it will distract from the primary subject-matter. Simple backgrounds can show your subject off to best effect.

Of course, these considerations of how to frame your shot tell only part of the story. They would apply equally well to your holiday snaps as a news picture. What about the editorial value of pictures? How can they contribute to your storytelling or tell stories of their own?

This extract by Bill Pierce on the 'Digital Journalist' web site offers a vivid insight into the work of the photojournalist – constantly evaluating the editorial content of each picture while also constructing the shot and getting it pinsharp:

> You zoom back and show the candidate against the flag. You try several frames with him at the edge of the frame. The frame on the flag is exact. And the depth-of-field preview shows that the flag is recognizable. The candidate starts to sweat under the heat of the television lights; so, you zoom in as tight as you can. You feel bad about not including the press secretary looking bored and eating Cheese Duds at the edge of the frame, but you're going for the impact colour cover, not the revealing side bar that will end up in the wastebasket. Wait a second, you've got a zoom and a motor. You zoom back just a hair and knock off just one frame that includes the bag of Cheese Duds. It won't make it into the mag, but it may be good for the contests.[3]

In this piece Pierce was in fact discussing the relative merits of two different cameras, but as an insight into the editorial power of the photojournalist, well . . . you get the picture.

---

[3] www.dirckhalstead.org

Moving pictures

You are more likely to offer still pictures than video on your site at the current time (2001). Downloading video is still not a user-friendly experience and unless you are an established broadcaster, the production quality you could bring to any home grown video is questionable, especially when viewed on the relatively low resolution of a PC monitor.

But while we're about it, let's offer some basic advice to avoid the 'video nasties'.

1 Carefully consider your subject and the surrounding area and try to frame each shot sequence.
2 Provide a focal point for each shot.
3 If you film someone and he or she is looking into the shot (i.e. on the right-hand side of frame, but looking towards the middle), make sure the subject stays in that position for the whole of the sequence/interview.
4 Avoid excessive zooming.
5 Avoid hand-held filming unless necessary. Invest in a tripod.
6 Make sure you have all the shots you need to provide a logical visual sequence when you edit them together. As well as your main interviews and sequences, you may require 'establishing' shots (e.g. the outside of a building where an interview is about to take place), 'cutaways' (general shots used to hide the joins between edits where otherwise the picture would jump from the end of one sequence to the start of another) and the dreaded 'noddies' (shots of interviewer nodding and maybe asking questions, recorded after the interview; these are used to mask edits in the interview or avoid questions being asked off-camera).
7 Make sure your audio is audible.
8 Whenever you can, use additional lighting.

Having looked in detail at how to collect news and information, we will now turn our attention to the third stage of the core journalistic process – the selection of material, prior to presentation.

Select

Calling selection a 'stage' could give the false impression that it is part of a sequence. In fact, many of the elements of the journalistic process should run concurrently. For example, the journalist should constantly be sifting through ideas from the beginning and making selections, always guided by the paramount considerations of what will interest, inform and have an impact on the readership or audience.

Journalists will sometimes make the job more difficult by delaying selection. They might follow too many leads and gather too much information. This undermines one of the most important responsibilities of the journalist, that is, to choose what the reader will and will not see. The journalist cannot carry out this function effectively if his or her mind is clouded by too much information.

Does the journalist still have the same responsibility in the online world, where the user is free to choose from millions of documents, sites and sources? The answer is 'Yes', as:

■ many of the documents posted on the Web are completed stories which will have required journalists to execute their traditional role, selecting what to include and what to exclude;
■ it will often be the journalist who selects additional information and data as part of any storytelling – again, choices will be made; and
■ even when links to original sources are offered, these will have been chosen by journalists.

Of course, if the online reader is unhappy with these choices, he or she can seek out additional perspectives, information and sources from the web on their own, for example, by using a search engine. But many won't. Instead, as Steve Yelvington said, they will rely on the journalist to be, if not the gatekeeper, at least the guide. And guides have to make choices.

Writing and constructing your story are two other critical elements of the selection and presentation of news and information. The Web remains fundamentally a text-driven medium. So the core skills of direct writing and clear story construction are of paramount importance. Indeed, they are so important that Chapters 4 and 5 are devoted to an examination of them. But the selection process extends to other areas such as multimedia. Here we will concentrate on audio, because it is more accessible for the online user.

Editing audio

This sounds like something you might do after the interview. Yet, in fact, you start the editing process when you initially research your story. If your preparation produces a more structured and focused interview, it will also probably be a shorter one. This is a form of editing.

With practice, you will also find yourself 'editing' in your head during the interview by ditching certain questions and changing lines of attack. Again, thorough preparation will give you more freedom to think this way during the interview. As a result, you will have less editing to do and a clearer idea of what should stay and what should go during the edit.

Without adequate preparation, the interview will probably end up as with a long, rambling conversation which travels down various cul-de-sacs and diversions. You will then be rewarded with a 'double whammy' when it comes to editing, particularly under pressure. The interview will have taken longer to conduct, so you have (1) less time to edit, but (2) more to listen to on play back. It will feel like events are conspiring against you. But they are not. Such difficulties are self-inflicted.

Whenever you are editing factual audio, the Golden Rules are:

- listen to the interview carefully first and only download what you need to edit;
- listen to the rhythm, pace, cadence and sound level of the voice(s) you are editing;
- always listen back to your edit before transmission; and
- *never* alter the sense or otherwise misrepresent what has been said by the interviewee.

The Golden Rules apply to both the main types of edits. These can be summarized as:

- editing an extract for transmission (getting an audio 'cut' or 'clip') then discarding the rest; and
- editing extracts to be discarded and transmitting the remainder (usually a full interview).

Each of these approaches has its own additional rules, some of which can apply to either category. If that sounds imprecise, it is. Editing is a combination of editorial judgement and technical skill; it is not an exact science.

When editing for cuts or clips, try to choose a cut where the interviewee is fluent, yet concise and direct (not always easy) and where he or she tackles one of the main issues or clearly explains his or her position on the issue. Avoid summarizing statements. Although politicians love these soundbites, they often appear contrived and stale.

On no account should you collude in this sterile exercise by asking the interviewee to 'give a 20-second clip on this' in place of a proper interview. In addition, you should avoid cuts that just list facts. These can be marshalled more concisely in your supporting text. When taking a quick clip, it is tempting to finish the edit mid-sentence. This is acceptable if it does not break a Golden Rule. Do not make the edit on a rising inflection in the voice, as it sounds unnatural.

When editing interviews, be bold. Do not get hung up with taking out every pause and hesitation. They are part of natural speech. Indeed, a pause indicating emotion, thought, indecision or ignorance should never be taken out. Instead, concentrate on removing the sentences or whole answers you do not want.

Rather than cutting from the bottom up (like a newspaper sub-editor), try to cut from within the piece to improve the flow and structure *but without altering the sense*. Note the rhythm of the speech. Leave breathing spaces both within and at the end of sentences. Otherwise you get 'tight edits' (words butted too close together). Remove any reference to material you have already edited ('as I said earlier') and anything that is inaudible (do not listen too often on headphones or you will convince yourself that something of borderline quality is acceptable – it may not be when transmitted).

Present

The final stage is the presentation. It is a fundamental element of the core journalistic process, but it is the one most tied into the medium within which you are working. Television demands pictures. Radio must be accessible. Online has its own distinctive qualities and demands.

As a result of this, there are few rules for presentation that can be applied across all media. You must make sure you work with the medium to tell your story most effectively and usefully to your readers/audience/users. Obviously, this directs how you structure your stories and use your editorial raw material. As we will see later in the book, online is no different in this respect.

However, online *is* unusual in that, as yet, there is little standardization of either product or delivery platform. In comparison, one television bulletin or news show looks similar to another. Convention drives presentation.[4]

There is a convention forming in the online community, but it is early days. In comparison to most other news media, web sites look and sometimes behave differently. Just when a consensus starts to form, along comes another level of technology, such as wireless or broadband, to raise more questions without answers and refuel the debate on how best to present information online.

This consensus vacuum is both unsettling and invigorating. It can stimulate innovation, but it can also lead to bad practice. Doing your own thing is not always a suitable spectator sport. And that's bad news if the purpose of 'your thing' is to communicate to others by presenting information online.

So what do people turn to in the absence of conventions? Often, it is core values – the stuff they know they can sign up to and still be free to find their own expression. 'We are still experimenting with how exactly we are going to do it, but this is what we want to do. This is our purpose.' That's why this book aims to extend the

---

[4] If there was ever doubt about this, it was put aside when Channel 5 news was launched in the UK (in 1997) with presenters walking the floor and leaning against desks. The resultant media stir said more about the conventional nature of British television than any revolutionary initiative on Channel 5's part.

core values and process of journalism through the structure of the
individual online story, to the larger expression of communicating
the message – web site design and all that entails. Journalism,
after all, is all about communication.

Further reading and references

Keeble, R. (1998). *The Newspaper Handbook*. Routledge.
Northmore, D. (1996). *Lifting the Lid*. Cassell.
Randall, D. (1999). *The Universal Journalist*. Pluto Press.

Journalism review sites:

- www.ajr.newslink.org – the site of the *American Journalism Review*. Articles, searchable archive, top ten sites and links to 3,700 news sources.
- www.americanreview.net – a critical review of US media.
- www.cjr.org – the online version of the *Columbia Journalism Review* from one of the United States' blue chip journalism departments. It covers journalism in every medium.

Professional/educational bodies:

- www.naa.org – the site of the Newspaper Association of America. Links, news, events and information.
- www.icfj.org – the site for the International Center For Journalists, which is dedicated to the professional development of journalists worldwide.
- www.poynter.org – one of the leading US journalism schools, which is particularly strong on professional updating.
- http://spj.org – the site the Society of Professional Journalists.

News sites:

- www.broadcast-live.com/newspapers/ – do not be misled by this URL for the Cyber Newstand of world newspapers.

- www.holdthefrontpage.co.uk – a useful resource on UK journalism.
- www.dirckhalstead.org – the site for the *Digital Journalist Magazine* on photojournalism in the digital age.
- www.interfax-news.com – the site of the Interfax News Agency. Political and business news from Russia, the CIS and the Baltic States.

Journalism standards:

- www.bbc.co.uk/info/editorial/prodgl/contents.htm – once upon a less complicated time, the BBC Producer Guidelines were contained in a slim volume you could slip into your coat pocket. Now they would give you a hernia to keep on your person. Thankfully, they are available online. Both a useful resource and fascinating insight into an organization that takes its journalism very seriously.
- www.fair.org – 'fair' stands for Fairness and Accuracy In Reporting, a self-explanatory acronym from this US-based media watchdog group.
- www.journalism.org – a stimulating site from the US-based Committee for Concerned Journalists, highlighting its Project for Excellence in Journalism.
- www.muckraker.org – despite the name, this site has a deeply serious purpose, housing the Centre for Investigative Reporting, which both conducts investigations and supports the training of others in this important area.
- www.uta.fi/ethicnet/ – a database of European codes of journalism ethics.

Beyond the UK and the United States:

- http://ejc.nl – born out of the energetic European Journalism Training Association, the European Journalism Centre is an independent forum for journalists around Europe. The site contains details of seminars, projects and training opportunities, and 'International Media News Daily' offers news on the latest developments in European and international media for the current and previous weeks.

- www.icij.org – the site of the International Consortium of Investigative Journalists.
- www.lanic.utexas.edu/la/region/journalism/ – Lanic: University of Texas resources for journalism in English, Spanish and Portuguese.
- www.markovits.com/journalism/ – a journalistic resources page on education and research in journalism. Good geographic spread of links.
- www.uow.edu.au/crearts/journalism/ – this site from the University of Wollongong's Graduate School of Journalism incorporates a link to the Asian Journalism Network.

Public relations resources:

- www.prcentral.com – PR Central. Online news and intelligence for professional communicators. The 'Body of Knowledge' link comprises archives, case histories and a bookstore.
- www.prnewswire.com – news from corporations worldwide for the media, business and financial community and the individual investor.
- www.prsa.org – the site of the Public Relations Society of America.
- www.usprnet.com – the National PR Network's site, where PR professionals exchange news, contacts and information.
- www.webcom.com/impulse/prlist.html – Public Relations Agencies and Resources on the Web.

3 Online research and reporting

> 'Just what do you think you're doing Dave? . . . I really think
> I'm entitled to an answer to that question.'
>
> *HAL* the shipboard computer in *2001: A Space Odyssey*[1]

Imagine you're climbing a mountain and getting instructions from someone who's reached the top. The top of the mountain is their perspective. So their advice and guidance uses references and terms which might be invaluable half-way up the cliff face. But they're less helpful when you are still huddled in your tent at base camp, staring at your feet.

There have been numerous attempts to define how journalists use online resources to assist their research and reporting. But they usually start from the top of the mountain, listing devices such as search engines, subject directories and Boolean logic before explaining what they can do. Many find the language alone deeply discouraging and retreat to their tents.

This chapter – in particular the way it is structured – is dedicated to the online tent dwellers, wherever you are, and so it will be 'bottom up' in its approach. It will consider how journalists implement the newsgathering process detailed in Chapter 2 and then it will explain some of the online tools that can help them to do it.

Online research and reporting is already a well-established journalistic discipline. People have written excellent books about

[1] *2001: A Space Odyssey* (1968). Directed by Stanley Kubrick.

single elements of it, such as data analysis. The aims of this chapter are modest – to demystify the process; to introduce several, but not all, of the key areas of online research; and hopefully to whet the appetite and encourage you to try it for yourself.

Too many people are deterred by their early forays online. If you were offered 24,853 web pages to look at, after putting your first simple query to a search engine, you are not likely to have progressed to the wonders of newsgroups, listservs or even data analysis (more language to daunt the faint hearted).

Turning your back on the Internet after an unhappy first encounter may be one way of handling a fear of the unknown, but it's dubious journalistic practice. The only remedy is to cut through the jargon, try things out, keep plugging away and see what works *for you*.

The impact of online on research and reporting

As we have seen, there are two main tasks for the journalist – the *gathering* of news materials and their *dissemination*. Researching and reporting form the 'gathering-in' process, the first two of the four stages detailed in Chapter 2. As we will see in this chapter, online can have a striking impact on this work, helping you trace information, come up with story ideas and find sources, contacts and potential interviewees.

Then come the latter stages of story construction and publishing, the selection and presentation of your information. That 'sending-out' or dissemination process, and how online makes it distinctive, will be covered in later chapters. In this chapter, we will concentrate on news gathering.

Four elements of 'gathering in'

Using the bottom-up approach, we can identify the main elements of research and reporting and consider how the use of online can support them.

- finding information – a broad heading, which could include documents, data, photographs, audio, video (these tend to be the more static artefacts);

- finding people – not just named individuals, but also tapping into debate, current thinking, trends and fashions (this is a more fluid grouping);
- checking information – using online reference resources; and
- analysing information – in particular, data.

These categories are not watertight. Some of the techniques used to find people, such as mailing lists, will also give you information. Similarly, looking on web pages for information will often lead to people. However, as reflections of the core journalistic activities, they will suffice, as long as we see them for what they are, namely entry points for the uninitiated, not definitive groupings. Once you get to know your way around, the finer differences will become apparent.

This chapter focuses on how to find information and people. More refined computer assisted reporting (CAR) techniques, such as data capture and analysis, form another important but specialized area, not well served by 'a brief introduction'. The use of spreadsheets by reporters to analyse information such as government statistics has become established in the United States. Reporters have been able to utilize existing data sets or compile their own and produce results that even the most innumerate journalist would immediately see had strong news value. As a result, trends, gaps, mistakes and cover-ups have been revealed. They have been there all the time, sitting in the data. It's just needed a journalist to ask the right questions, run the right sequence of numbers.

However, many journalists outside the United States are prone to CARsickness. For example, as yet, there is little evidence of the more advanced CAR techniques being used in the UK, partly because of the difficulty journalists feel they face getting the raw data. It's easy to exaggerate the divide between the US and the rest of the world in relation to CAR. Nora Paul has been one of the leading advocates of the benefits of CAR. She has spoken of the 'mythology of the United States being so advanced in everything computer related'. She has seen a gradual growth among US journalists in the regular use of spreadsheets to analyse city budgets and similar material. 'But if you are talking about major, month-long, big series, heavy analysis, it's still a very small proportion of US newsrooms that invest in that.'[2]

Paul talks about the 'gradations of CAR'. She points out that simply using the Internet to find people and information is one form of computer assisted reporting and that this is becoming widespread among reporters in the UK and other countries outside the United States. She also suggests that UK journalists could look beyond the big government data sets and compile their own material:

> Over time you might compile individual incidents. These cumulatively may reveal certain trends ... data about production, or trade or economic issues or the Royal budget is absolutely within the power of UK journalism and I think that's starting to be seen.

Sources of information on CAR are listed at the end of this chapter.

Finding information – the World Wide Web

You need information at every stage of the news identification and collection process. Not just specific information to develop your story, but contextual stuff that will bolster your knowledge of underpinning structures and current affairs.

Much of the information available online is posted on the World Wide Web. Recent studies put the number of documents on the Web at over one billion, and this is estimated to grow to over 13 billion pages by 2004.

This is where the trouble starts. Such quantities rattle the senses. You literally do not know where to begin and there is further discouragement. The Web is not like a library and it does not have a single comprehensive catalogue or an ordered system of storage.

So what do you do? You take a deep breath and start to look for the different sorts of order that exist within the apparent chaos.

---

[2] Interview with author, June 2000.

When confronted with a keyboard, a screen and a fantastically sophisticated plaything like the Web, the overwhelming urge is to dive in. This is fine and you should indulge yourself. But, then switch off your computer before it switches you off. At an early stage, learn to think as clearly as possible about what you are looking for *before* you go online.

Types of web site

First, if it helps, think of the different kinds of site that exist on the web and make a list. You will see that like any collection, you can introduce categories, such as those suggested in Chapter 1. That alone begins to reduce the Web to more manageable proportions (no, don't stop to think how many documents are in each of your categories, it's pointless).

Uniform resource locators and domains

Next, all sites have an address, which is known as the uniform resource locator (URL). Every page on every site will have its own distinctive address with the site URL as its root.

So the URL for the BBC site is bbc.co.uk. If you want the main weather page, the URL is bbc.co.uk/weather.

URLs have a great deal to answer for. They are responsible for the dreaded 'dotcom' entering our vocabulary (.com is the ending of the web addresses for many of the recent Internet start-up companies). They are also the bane of broadcasters' lives as they labour on air through 'wwws' and 'forward slashes', cross-trailing web sites on television and radio.

However, URLs do have their uses. Once you know the URL of a site, you can ask your computer to 'bookmark' it ('bookmark' is usually on the toolbar at the top of the page or 'favourites' if you use Internet Explorer). It will then be added to a list of stored sites that you can return to in the future without further searching. If a site changes its URL, it will usually leave a link to its new URL on the old page (a little like forwarding mail).

URLs are also like postal addresses because they can say something about the person or organization that resides there.

The secret lies in the suffix (section at the end) known as the 'domain'. It is worth familiarizing yourself with the key domain names because they can help you both identify and find web sites and pages.

Domains are split into two key areas – one denotes geography, the other signals the main purpose of the organization.

We have already mentioned .com. This simply stands for 'commercial' and denotes that the site in question is probably, but not always, a business or commercial venture. Dotcoms started in the United States, but have spread beyond, to the UK in particular.

Other domains that denote the purpose of the organization include:

■ .co.uk, which is UK commercial;
■ .edu, which is education;
■ .ac.uk, which is UK higher education;
■ .gov, which is government;
■ .int, which is international organizations;
■ .mil, which is US Department of Defense;
■ .net, which is networks; and
■ .org, which is non-commercial organizations.

The geographical codes are often more clear cut, for example .au is Australia and .ca is Canada. However, some would be more difficult to guess. Neither Portugal (.pt) or Poland (.pl) have the code .po (Po is in fact is a Tellytubby with a purple friend called Tinky Winky).

As can be seen from the list above, some domains combine the two. The University of Central Lancashire is a University in the UK. Its URL is uclan.ac.uk. If we break that down we can see the following:

■ uclan. (University of Central Lancashire);
■ ac.(University domain); and
■ uk (uk domain).

In this instance 'ac' denotes the purpose and 'uk' denotes the geographical location. So just by examining a simple URL such as this, we could have a fairly accurate guess of where it came from.

This is valuable when you are trying to find a site or when you have a URL and are trying to ascertain who it belongs to (you may not have a PC to hand at the time). It is also a simple but effective first lesson in demystifying the Web.

So you are looking for a specific web site and know the name of the organization that hosts it, you can try to guess the URL. For example, if you wanted the site of 'Ward's Wonder Widgets', you could try each of the following into the white address box near the top of your page:

- www.wardswonderwidgets.com;
- www.wardswidgets.com; or
- www.wonderwidgets.com.

Web site addresses often use initials. So in this case, you could also try the key sticking www.www.com (the initial www stands for World Wide Web).

If you know that Ward's Wonder Widgets are based in the UK, you can replace the suffix .com with .co.uk in any of the above instances.

How to look further

So now you know there are many different forms of document on the web but that each can be identified by its URL. You could carry on bookmarking ones you know and trying to guess others, but to leave it there would be to see only a single snowflake on the tip of this iceberg of information. To discover the true value of the web as a resource, you will have to search it.

Before you do this, you must ask yourself two important 'bottom-up' questions.

- What type of information am I looking for? Deconstruct the potential story and look at its component parts. What sort of information, opinion and data will help to develop the story or help to brief you?

■ Where am I likely to find it? Can the web sites you already know and trust give you the information you need? If they cannot, you should consider which search tool will be the most appropriate and efficient.

Search tools

In the same way as many people confuse the Internet and the web, some confuse search tools and search engines. Search engines are one way of searching the Web, but they are not the only search tool. There are others that can be more effective depending on what you need.

Again, we can use the bottom-up approach. Instead of listing the different search tools and then describing what they are most appropriate for, we can consider a number of possible scenarios faced by researching journalists and then suggest the best search tool. (An explanation of how each works will follow.)

1 You want information about a specific individual or an organization and you have their name. Try a search engine.
2 You are looking for a specific document and the guesswork hasn't worked. Try a search engine.
3 You have a specific query, but you want to get a fast overview of what might available on the web. Try a meta search engine.
4 You are researching a broader area, rather than making a specific query. It may be your initial search on the topic. Try a subject directory.
5 You want to narrow your topic area and go into more depth, maybe looking for expert opinion and informed sources. Try a subject guide.

With practice, you learn how to use a combination of these search tools when seeking information. But for now, we can consider them individually.

Search engines
Search engines are hugely powerful pieces of software that search for web content. You will normally find a list of search engines offered on your browser when you log on to the Net.

Some examples of search engines are:

- AltaVista (www.altavista.com) or its sister engine Raging Search (raging.com);
- Google (www.google.com);
- Hotbot (www.hotbot.com); and
- Northern Light (www.northernlight.com).

(Note: the URLs do not contain many surprises.)

Each engine provides a box to type in the 'keywords' of the material you are looking for. Your choice of these keywords plays a large part in the success of your search. Normally, the engine will scan web pages looking for meta data that matches your keywords. Meta data is part of the HTML code for each web page, inserted by the page's author but hidden from view unless you look for it. If you want to see what HTML, including meta data, looks like, open a web page using your web browser, click on the 'View' option on your toolbar and then 'Source'. What you will then see is all the HTML used to make that one web page. Much of the HTML will be describing how the information on the page should be organized but some of it will be information about the page itself, including date, subject, author and content description. This is the meta data.

If the engine thinks the page is one you want, it will add it to a list and show you it, together with the hypertext link to take you to the actual page and site.

The most important thing to understand about search engines is that they are all different. The more you know about their differences, the greater will be your success when you use them.

Search engines do not scour the web 'live' when you make a query. Instead, they search large databases of web pages they have compiled. Different engines have different sizes of databases, frequency of updating and methods of indexing. They also have different methods of searching.

However, considering that the Web currently has an estimated billion pages, no search engine will look everywhere on the Web.

Search engines also have different features. They are too many and varied to describe here, but again the lesson is clear. Find out about your search engine. The few examples below illustrate the very different features you can now find on search engines.

- Google ranks its search returns by calculating how often pages have been linked to other popular sites, rather than just how often the key search word or phrase appears on the pages in question.
- Ask Jeeves (which in fact is a meta search engine – see below) has a vast library of questions to which it knows the 'answer' in terms of a search return. It allows you to put a question in plain English, rather than entering key words or phrases, and then tries to match your question to one of its own answers.
- Users of Northern Light can search not only the web database but also its own online business library (but you pay for articles from this special section).

Figure 3.1: Google is one of the best search engines. Note the simplicity of the initial interface, inviting you to try the search function. However, your results will depend on how well you refine your search request. (Google Brand Features are trademarks of Google, Inc.)

Results from search engines can vary markedly. Figures from the University of California at Berkeley's library site[3] indicate that submitting very comparable searches to different search engines can produce about a 40% variation on search results, with about 60% of the results listing the same sites.

Meta search engines

Although this sounds like a further step down the dark road of jargon, a meta search engine is in fact a simple concept. It is a search engine that harnesses the power of other search engines. It searches the other search engines, rather than building its own database.

If this sounds like a reason for ignoring the individual search engines and heading straight for the Big One, here first is a word of caution.

According to the Berkeley Library site:

Most meta-search engines only spend a short time in each database and often retrieve only 10% of any of the results in any of the databases queried. This makes their searches usually 'quick and dirty' but often good enough to find what you want.

Also, how well will the different search engines understand the terms of your single, original search request submitted to the original meta search engine?

However, meta search engines are usually fast and if you know the specific term or phrase you are looking for, they are a good way of getting a quick overview of what is on offer.

Importantly, they also give you the opportunity to comb through the contents of both search engines and subject directories (see below) simultaneously.

Some meta-search engines are:

■ Dogpile (www.dogpile.com);
■ Inference Find (www.infind.com);

[3] www.lib.berkeley.edu

Figure 3.2: Digging deep for gold: The whole world should know about Vivian Stanshall, but sadly it does not. Meta search engines such as Dogpile can be useful when you are exploring off the beaten path, as you get a top slice of results from many different engines. Note the variance in results listed at the top of the page. (Reprinted with express permission of InfoSpace, Inc. All rights reserved.)

REM charity auction
on Yahoo! Auctions

BID WITH STAR TREK™ YAHOO!

Yahoo! Mail
Y! Chat, Y! Messenger

| Search | advanced search

You are searching: ⊙ All of Yahoo!   ○ UK only   ○ Ireland only

Yahoo! Messenger - Instant, customisable, communication!

Shop · Auctions · Shopping · Property · **Jobs** · Cars · Business Finder · **Media** · News · **Sport** · Finance · Ski · TV · Weather
Connect · Chat · **Clubs** · GeoCities · Greetings · Invites · UK Email · IE Email · Messenger · Mobile · People Search
Personal · My Yahoo! · Address Book · Calendar · Briefcase · Bookmarks · **Companion** · Photos · Horoscopes · **more...**

Yahoo! Auctions Bid, buy or sell anything!

Categories		Items	
· Comic Books	· Electronics	· PlayStation	· REM
· Coins	· Science Fiction	· MP3 Players	· Help a London Child
· Computers	· Stamps	· Mobile Phones	· Star Trek
· DVD's	· Travel	· PDA's	· Oxfam

Arts & Humanities
Literature, Photography...

Business & Economy
B2B, Shopping, Investments, Taxes...

Computers & Internet
Internet, WWW, Software, Games...

Education
UK, Ireland, Universities...

Entertainment
Humour, Movies, Music, Cool Links...

Government
UK, Ireland, Europe, Politics...

Health
Medicine, Drugs, Diseases, Fitness...

News & Media
Full Coverage, Newspapers, TV...

Recreation & Sport
Sport, Outdoors, Travel, Motoring...

Reference
Libraries, Dictionaries, Phone Numbers...

Regional
UK, Ireland, Countries, Regions...

Science
CS, Biology, Astronomy, Engineering...

Social Science
Anthropology, Sociology, Economics...

Society & Culture
People, Environment, Royalty, Religion...

powered by COMPAQ

In the News
· Palace braced as 'Sophie tapes' are published
· Foot-and-mouth: Cull appeals 'undermining firebreak strategy'
· U.S. plane crew start second week in Chinese detention
· Former Beatle to sell home after attack
· Off your chops? Tune in to TV's "Pig Brother"
· **Sport**: Football - Cricket: W.Indies v S.Africa · Tennis · Golf - US Masters
more...

Marketplace
· Computers, electronics & music on Y! Shopping
· Insurance - Motor · Life · Travel · Home - get quotes, tips, more
· Get a new job with Y! Employment

Events
· Win a holiday to the British Virgin Isles!
· 1.30 - 10.30pm :Daily sports radio show!

Inside Yahoo!
· Latest on Eastenders, Corrie, Brookie & more on Y! Soaps
· Icons, ringtones & WAP services on Y! Mobile
· Y! Photos - upload, share & order prints

Figure 3.3: Yahoo!, as a directory, presents a very different interface compared to a search engine (see Figure 3.1). It categorizes content into subject headings, inviting the visitor to browse (although you can also search Yahoo). (Reproduced with permission of Yahoo! Inc. © 2000 by Yahoo! Inc. YAHOO! and the YAHOO! logo are trademarks of Yahoo! inc.)

■ Metacrawler (www.metacrawler.com); and
■ ProFusion.com (www.profusion.com).

Subject directories

Some people might name their favourite search engine as Yahoo!, but Yahoo! is a subject directory not a search engine (although it has now teamed up with the Google search engine to offer both facilities on its site).

Making this distinction is not pedantry. It is actually quite important. Subject directories are put together in a fundamentally different way to search engines. You need to be aware of the difference to know which one to use and when.

Most search engines use software to comb through millions of web pages, looking for traces of your key search word. Yahoo!, as a subject directory, has been compiled by human beings. This means you can browse through a database of handpicked sites organized under subject headings (in much the same way as you would browse books in different sections of a library). You can search it too. You tend to be offered web sites, whereas search engines hunting for your key word, will pick up individual web pages.

Like most things in life, the intervention of humans brings advantages and disadvantages to subject directories. Extraneous, coincidental yet irrelevant material tends to be filtered out so you can get a higher quality of information. Yet, inevitably, the database is usually smaller. This reduces the number of search returns, and also takes them from a smaller sample, which is probably less up-to-date.

Examples of subject directories include:

■ Britannica's best web sites (www.britannica.com);
■ Galaxy (www.galaxy.com); and
■ Yahoo! (www.yahoo.com) (with a UK version called uk.yahoo.com).

Again, please note. Still no surprises among the URLs.

Restricted area search tools

The subject headings in Yahoo! are many and varied, covering most areas of human endeavour – everything from arts, humanities and business through to health and science. So they are useful for the early broad search.

However, sometimes you want to limit your initial search, perhaps by country or by subject-matter. In that case, a restricted area search tool can be a useful alternative. For example, www.ukplus.co.uk is useful for UK-based material or ananzi.com is valuable for South African web sites.

There are also search tools that concentrate on one subject area only, for example:

- www.findlaw.com, with a focus on legal matters; and
- www.healthfinder.gov, which is a comprehensive site for health information.

Subject guides

These are rather like the restricted subject area search tools listed above. They are usually web sites run by individual experts in their fields. They focus on a single subject and contain many links to other relevant sites and some useful additional information, comment and evaluation by the site provider. They can also put you in touch with the best online discussion groups in their particular sector (see 'Mailing lists' and 'Newsgroups' later in this chapter).

Subject guides can be a valuable 'one stop shop' starting point for reporters specializing in a certain field. But how do you find them? You could look for them using a search engine or they may even be listed in Yahoo! as individual entries.

But there are also some useful sites which act as clearing houses and directories for specialist subject guides. They not only group the subject guides together, but also evaluate them before including them in their online directory. Examples of clearing houses are:

- Argus Clearinghouse (www.clearinghouse.net); and
- WWW Virtual Library (www.vlib.org).

Some journalists and journalism schools have developed sites that have become useful subject guides for reporters and researchers. A few examples are:

The Internet's Premier Research Library
A Selective Collection of Topical Guides

The**Argus**Clearinghouse

Navigation	Categories

Search/Browse

Arts & Humanities

Internet Searching
Center

Business & Employment

Communication

Computers & Information Technology

Site Information

Education

FAQ

Engineering

Submit a Guide

Environment

Digital Librarian's
Award

Government & Law

Ratings System

Health & Medicine

Contact Us

Places & Peoples

Recreation

Science & Mathematics

Social Sciences & Social Issues

Figure 3.4: The Argus Clearinghouse is one of the best places to find specialist subject guides.

- www.PowerReporting.com
- www.NewsDesk-UK.com
- CARpark-UK (www.rawlinson.co.uk)
- www.ejta.org (the European journalists' site); and
- www.journalismnet.org (no list would be complete without Julian Sher's humungous collection of journalism links, including sections for different countries).

How to look for information

Have you ever been embarrassed by your ignorance of a foreign language? When abroad, are you like Basil Fawlty? Do you repeat the same word in English over and over again, only louder, desperate to be understood? You are in a shop and you want some bread. The shop assistant brings you toothbrushes, soap, milk – anything but bread.

That's what search tools feel like when confronted by an inexperienced searcher. They see a Basil. They want to help. They will bring you anything they think will help. But unless you learn their language, they will probably disappoint you and like Basil, that will make you very cross indeed.

Search language is not difficult to learn. The simplest refinements to basic search questions can significantly improve your returns from engines and directories and, unlike Basil Fawlty, get you nearer to what you want.

The best way to refine your search is to narrow it by being specific. The easiest way to do that is to use a cross-referencing system. For example, if you ask an engine to look for information on 'Frank Zappa', you will get a huge return. If you ask it to cross reference its search for Zappa with the term 'Mothers of Invention', you will get a more focused return of Zappa material from the days when he fronted his band the Mothers of Invention. If you then cross reference it further and ask it to look for 'Frank Zappa', the 'Mothers of Invention' and 'Ian Underwood', you will probably get material focused on the keyboard and sax genius (they were all geniuses) Ian Underwood during his time in the band with Zappa. So you can use the cross-reference to include multiple subjects which act as filters.

Figure 3.5: This site (www.journalismnet.com), produced by the indefatigable Julian Sher, is a goldmine of web resources. This is part of the front page of the UK section.

You can also use the same system to exclude categories. For example, if you wanted to check if Ian Underwood had ever worked with Frank Zappa outside of the Mothers of Invention, you could ask the engine to add Zappa and Underwood but subtract, or exclude, the Mothers of Invention. Instead of adding, you are taking away. It is still simple arithmetic.

The difficulty, if any, comes in phrasing these addition and subtraction commands so that the many different kinds of search engine and directories understand your requirements.

This should be a cue for George Boole and his Logic (sounds like another band). But let's meet someone else first. His name is Danny Sullivan. He is the editor of www.searchenginewatch.com, which is one of the best sites for information on search tools. This site is not only comprehensive, but also accessible. Danny has a simple message for the uninitiated:

> Forget about power searching. Don't worry about learning to do a 'Boolean' search. All most people need to know is a little basic 'search engine math(s)' in order to improve their results . . . learn how to easily add, subtract and multiply your way into better searches at your favourite search engine. (It) works for nearly all the major search engines.[4]

And that goes for subject directories too.

Simple arithmetic

Search engine maths uses the + and – symbols, with a few extras to do your cross-referencing for you.

Go to www.searchenginewatch.com/facts/math.html for the full details. But we can use the Frank Zappa example here by way of brief explanation.

To find the Frank Zappa pages from his time with the band the Mothers of Invention, you could search this way:

+zappa +mothers

---

[4] www.searchenginewatch.com

(You must leave a single space between the first complete keyword +zappa and the next +mothers, but there is no gap between the + sign and the keyword.)

This search will give you pages from Zappa's time with the Mothers of Invention. It may produce references to Zappa and mothers of children, but you can iron out that wrinkle in a minute when you have learned multiplication.

If you want to find documents that refer to Zappa, the Mothers of Invention and Ian Underwood, you could try:

+zappa +mothers +underwood

As mentioned above, using the − symbol, you can exclude references. So to continue with the Frank Zappa example, you could look for Zappa and Underwood collaborating outside the Mothers of Invention by asking for:

+zappa +underwood −mothers

To look for Ian Underwood activity away from Frank Zappa and the Mothers of Invention, you could try:

+underwood −zappa −mothers

Now we can consider the multiplication of some terms. If you wanted to ensure that you received only references to the Mothers of Invention and not the maternal breed in general, you could multiply the words Mothers of Invention together to ensure that only words occurring together, in that order, would be picked up by the search. This is done by quotation marks.

So a more targeted initial search would be:

+zappa +"mothers of invention"

Better still would have been 'Frank Zappa', if, on this occasion, you did not also want material about his son, Dweezil, or any other Zappa who might have a link with the band.

This raises a crucially important point. It's easy to get carried away with such power searching. It can take on a life of its own. However, to serve its purpose, i.e. to inform your research and content creation, it must be directed by journalistic skills and informed by your subject knowledge. For example, while conducting this search you would also need to know that two Underwoods played with Zappa – Ian and Ruth. So if you are looking for Ian you need:

+zappa +"ian underwood"

Again, go to the source, Danny Sullivan, for more on this, including a list of search engines that will support search engine maths (most of them) and details of those where there may be some anomalies.

Let's now return briefly to George Boole. Search engine maths is an implied Boolean Logic. It is not using the same terms as the Boolean system (named after Boole, who was a nineteenth century British mathematician), but it has the same results.

Boolean terms (or 'operators') include:

- AND (same as +);
- NOT (same as –);
- OR (operated automatically by most search engines if you leave a space between search words and mainly used for synonymous terms, e.g. dogs OR canines would produce pages that had references to dogs or canines or both).

There's nothing wrong with using Boolean Logic but the term itself can place a barrier between the uninitiated and attempts at successful searching. It sounds mysterious, exotic even, but it's actually rather mundane, albeit useful. However, it does not operate identically across the different search engines. Until you know your favourite engine well enough to do advanced searches with the right operators, why not try simple addition, subtraction and multiplication?

Simple guiding principles for searching online

1 As noted above, stop and think about what you are looking for before you touch a keyboard. Is it a general search or a specific query? Do you want a particular document or details about a

named individual? If a general topic, does it have distinctive words or phrases? This will give you a helpful pointer to the search engines or directories you should use.[5]

2 Remember, as we discovered in the Zappa example, that any online search you conduct is not a 'stand alone'. It is an integral part of your journalism. You still need the underpinning knowledge of current affairs, political structures, etc, to put your questions into context and to make sense of the answers you receive. A lot of this will come from 'traditional' sources, such as newspapers, books and yes, even people.

3 If you do use a search engine, go to the 'Help' page first. You may believe that 'Help' pages are the preserve of those sad cases who actually learn how to master the 57 different functions of their DVD player. You're a 'plug it in and switch it on' sort of person. Resist this urge. Search engines are getting better at explaining just what they can do for the average (i.e. non-geek) punter. As many engines are different, it is worth finding out how they work. You do not have to learn the manual, just enough to make the engine or directory, rather than you, do the hard work.

4 Be patient. If you look for quick results from your searches and do not get them, don't downgrade the need to learn as a priority. 'It takes too long', 'I haven't got time to wade through all this stuff' and 'I've managed fine without it before' are the stock responses of the hard-pressed and frustrated journalist when he or she gets poor results from an online search. But that's a road to nowhere. Instead, try tinkering with search techniques in your own time when the pressure is off and persevere.

5 Most importantly, remember that seeing is not believing. Just because it's on a screen, it does not mean that it's true. Even 'official' sites can occasionally be hoaxes. Certainly anything homemade should be treated with caution. The Internet is the favourite playground of pranksters and mischief-makers. Supposed e-mail 'discussions' between groups can be the work of an individual. At times, it's a world of smoke and mirrors. Sites

---

[5] See the Berkeley Library site (www.lib.berkeley.edu) for a useful tutorial on developing search strategies.

with phone numbers and postal addresses are preferable to those with e-mail addresses only. Even so, double source and check all your findings independently whenever possible.

Simple tips for faster searching

1 Once you have mastered a search engine, it is still worth trying to guess the URL first if you know the name of the organization you are looking for. It can save a lot of time.

2 When looking through a long document retrieved by a search tool, press Control and F on your keyboard. This will offer you a box into which you can type your keyword. Hit the return key and you will be shown the place in the document where your keyword occurs if it is in the actual text rather than just the meta tag.

3 If you are opening several retrieved documents simultaneously, do not forget the right-hand key on your mouse. If you point the mouse at the 'back' button on Netscape or Explorer and hold down the right-hand mouse key, it will give you a menu of already opened pages to choose from, rather than having to laboriously click through each page in sequence with the left-hand key. Also, if pages are taking time to open, you can point to them, hit the right key and choose the 'Open in New Window' option and then move on to another. You can then hit the Alt and Tab keys to view what you have stored.

4 If you are looking for a word but want to cover alternative spellings, plurals, etc., use a wildcard. If you put the * symbol after the root, or beginning of the word, you will get all the words that begin with that root on certain major search engines such as Alta Vista. So, for example, customi* will get you customise and customize.

5 Looking for information specific to one country can be difficult. You can enter the name of the country as a keyword. However, how many documents originating from Denmark will have the word 'Denmark' written in them? Instead, find a search engine that will allow you to search by domain. Enter the subject of your search then (in the case of Alta Vista) domain: dk and you will receive all the documents on that subject originating from web sites with Danish domains. You can also search for the

domains describing organizations such as .org or even those that combine country and organization such as .ac.uk.

6 Know when to stop looking. There is a limit to how much time you should spend on any individual search or story.

So now you've stopped looking for information, let's look for people.

Electronic mail

You will find millions of people while you are searching for information. Virtually every web site will have an e-mail contact who can give you more information, expertise, etc. Electronic mail (e-mail) is the most frequently used application of the Internet. Current estimates put the number of users at over a hundred million and growing every day.

E-mail is a great tool for researchers and reporters (see Chapter 1 for distinctive features of e-mail), but it can have the following drawbacks.

■ You can spend hours looking for a person's e-mail address when two phone calls might put you in touch more quickly – one to check his or her company's phone number, the second to make the call. Do not become e-mail obsessed.

■ Busy people are snowed under with e-mails. The committed will take the trouble to respond, but some do not have time to read them right away.

■ Treat e-mail with caution. The name on the screen may not be the person who sent the message. Double check and source material independently, particularly if you want to quote something from an e-mail. As Nora Paul put it, 'I imagine when those new-fangled telephones first started being used in newsrooms, the old timers said, 'How can you believe you're really talking to the person they say they are, you can't see them!' A similar healthy scepticism is being voiced about using e-mail as a way to contact and interview people.'[6]

[6] www.poynter.org/car/cg-caremail.htm

Tracing e-mail addresses

Just like a web address URL, you can tell quite a lot from an e-mail address. There are four main components to any e-mail address. For example, meward@uclan.ac.uk is the address for my e-mail box at my place of work, the University of Central Lancashire in the UK. To break it down:

- meward is the user name;
- @ stands for 'at' – this separates the user name from the rest of the e-mail address;
- uclan is the computer at my place of work (u is University, c is Central, lan is Lancashire) which hosts my e-mail box; and
- ac.uk is the domain for British Universities.

Although it is worth trying to guess a web site URL, it is not as easy for e-mail. The problem lies with the user name. You might be able to guess or find out the name of the host computer and the domain, but there are different systems for user names.

Some host computers use initials and surnames, some use first names and surnames. Some put a full stop between the first name and the surname. Some do not.

Also, what happens if there is more than one Mike Ward with an e-mail box on the host computer to which you are sending the e-mail? Then the user name will usually have a number after it and you would need to know that number. If you were sending to John Smith, would he be j.smith1, j.smith5 or j.smith25?

So guessing an e-mail address can be fraught with difficulty, particularly if the person in question only has a private mail box. However, if that person works for an organization and for some reason you cannot trace him or her by telephone, try the following:

- go the organization's web site;
- see if the individual's e-mail address is listed on the site (the 'about us' or 'contacts' sections are good places to look if the site does not have a search function);
- if the person is not there, scrutinize the e-mail addresses of those who are there, noting the host computer name and

domain and the style of the user name (whether they use initials, etc.);

- guess the user name, using the appropriate style, and send an exploratory mail ('Looking for . . . sorry if this goes to wrong person, etc.); as you are treading on the edge of spamming (sending unsolicited and unwanted messages), only resort to this when all else fails and make sure you have a legitimate purpose;
- you might get lucky or you might get another person in the organization with the same/similar name, who is used to getting the wrong calls and e-mails and who will probably wearily re-direct you to your source.

There are other ways to trace e-mail addresses. There are now a number of web sites which act as large directories for e-mail addresses. As none is complete, try a combination of them. Again, try variations on user names, especially on the directories that require an exact match for a successful query, for example:

- www.bigfoot.com
- www.infospace.com/info/email1.htm
- www.worldemail.com/
- www.people.yahoo.com/

How secure is e-mail?

People are very trusting about e-mail. They type a message and send it out into cyberspace. It usually gets to its intended destination, but does it stop off anywhere on the way?

The answer is 'Yes'. The message will wend its way via your computer to the server that provides you with an Internet link and then to your correspondent's server and finally to you correspondent's computer. What you might not realize is that your message can stay on those servers for some time . . . and is retrievable.

So sending e-mail is not like having a private conversation with someone. You should always be careful what you commit to e-mail and never send them in anger. Think first, then send.

Tracing experts online

Sometimes you are not looking for a named individual, but someone, anyone, who has a certain expertise. The key lies not in who they are, but what they know.

Journalists working off-line will frequently phone their local university for an 'expert' view on a latest invention or government report. The reporter could be seeking background briefing or 'on the record' reaction and comment. The problem arises when the university has no-one willing or able to help.

Online journalists can extend their search by contacting www.profnet.com, which puts them in touch with an international network of over 11,000 news and information officers at colleges and universities, corporations, laboratories, medical centres and government agencies. The journalist states his or her query and it is distributed around the system. The appropriate experts are then asked to contact the journalist.

Other examples of resources for expert advice:

- www.earl.org.uk/ask/index.html (this UK-based site allows you to quiz librarians)
- www.askanexpert.com
- www.cvcp.ac.uk

Nora Paul also points out that sites such as Amazon.com can be used to trace authors who may be 'expert' in their fields. Similarly, you can trace specialist writers through magazines listed in www.mediafinder.com or www.publist.com.

Resources like Profnet have become so popular that some journalists have warned against their over-use. The reporter can become over-reliant on such a good source and become lazy and reactive – see a story, think of a possible follow-up and find an 'expert' to back it up.

Keeping your electronic ear to the ground

The journalist, particularly the specialist, must also keep in touch with current issues by listening to debate and tracking trends and issues. It is better to be ahead of the game than reacting to coverage in other media.

Internet applications have the potential to revolutionize this area of research and reporting. Previously, the journalist would have to subscribe to specialist printed journals and then write, fax or phone the authors of articles. Now they can monitor a constant stream of debate and discussion within specialist online communities. They can also contribute to the debate and contact other contributors by e-mail for further research and interviews.

There are two main meeting places for such online communities. They are:

■ mailing lists (also known as listservs); and
■ newsgroups (a confusing title as often they do not deal in news in the traditional sense).

Mailing lists

These are probably more productive than newsgroups for most journalists. Their content is often of a higher standard and more focused. They operate on an e-mail system. Groups of people with a similar academic or professional interest will form an e-mail mailing list. Each day, everyone on the list receives messages from anyone in the group who makes a contribution. Such messages usually stay within the e-mail system and are not posted on the web. However, some can be archived there and so are not always as private as you might imagine.[7]

To join a group, where you can 'lurk' (read without making a contribution) or post material yourself, you must send a carefully worded message to the mailing list's host computer. If accepted, you will be warned about the two different ways of messaging – one way is to the host computer, for example to cancel your subscription to the list; the other is for posting actual messages on the list. For some reason, to get them the wrong way round (i.e. send a service message to the other subscribers) is

[7] You can see the mailing list in action via the web, if you visit Steve Outing's site (www.planetarynews.com). You can use this as a gateway to access mailing lists for online news and online newspapers. The site is a valuable all-round resource, thinktank, discussion point and watering hole for content providers.

Online-Writing

Discussion list for those who write, edit and produce for the online medium

Read Messages

Messages are available from 2000/04/08 - 2001/04/08
These messages are from 03/28/01 - 04/08/01

[View Message]

```
The writing Lawyer needed... please. - 2001/04/08 [PAUL PAVLIK]
Education (Was re: ideas vs. implementation) - 2001/04/08 [Brandi Jasmine]
The value of university education (was Re: Ideas versus implementation (of...
Pay / Salary / Hourly Rates - 2001/04/07 [Peter Cooper]
Re: Ideas versus implementation (offtopic?) - 2001/04/07 [Peter Cooper]
—> Larry Phillips
Re: Ideas versus implementation - 2001/04/07 [Mark Neely]
—> Brandi Jasmine
re: ideas vs. implementation - 2001/04/06 [Sherry Darr]
—> Sherry Darr
Re: Ideas versus implementation (was Re: Rich Gordon's provocative view ...
Re: Ideas versus implementation (was Re: Rich Gordon's provocative view (lo...
Re: Ideas versus implementation (was Re: Rich Gordon's provocative view (...
Re: Ideas versus implementation (was Re: Rich Gordon's provocative view (l...
Ideas versus implementation (was Re: Rich Gordon's provocative view (long)...
```

[Jump Backward] [200 ▼]

Search for: ⦿ any or ◯ all of these words:
[   ] [Search]
⦿ entire message ◯ Body ◯ Header

Number of messages: [200 ▼] [threaded by subject ▼] [Show]

[   ] [Jump To Date] (Date in YYYY/MM/DD format, e.g., 1996/4/21)

[Main Menu]

● *Home*   LYRIS

Figure 3.6: Mailing list discussions usually run on e-mail only and so are not open to everybody on the web. However, if you want an insight into the kind of debate they can generate, you can read messages from the online-writing mailing list via the Poynter Institute's website – http://talk.poynter.org/online-news

unforgivable, to judge from the dire warnings on some mailing lists' subscriber information. Don't be put off by the tone of these warnings. Once inside, the natives of mailing lists are often friendly.

Of course, there are ways to make the natives restless. Mailing lists are not effective quick-fix solutions for journalists. For example, a reporter who crashed into a Grateful Dead mailing list seeking reaction from fans shortly after Jerry Garcia's death was apparently given very short shrift.

Yet as a tool for monitoring informed and current discussion in specific areas and also tracing contacts, they can be useful and you will not find only dry academics and ivory tower experts. Mailing lists dealing with community issues such as health and education may also have contributions from the grass roots – the real people, such as sufferers of certain illnesses or the parents of children with particular learning difficulties. These people can be invaluable contacts and sources.

Once again, Nora Paul[8] has good advice on the 'netiquette' of using mailing lists, but here are some quick and simple do's and don'ts:

- always identify yourself as a journalist;
- do not quote any mailing list contributions without permission;
- mailing lists are a publishing form, so watch out for the danger of libel; and
- do not allow your questions to give away any scoops you may have.

The most commonly used index of mailing lists is the web site called www.liszt.com. Here you will find mailing lists grouped under headings, like a subject directory. You can browse or search. Once again, the more precise the search request, the better the returns. If you spot a mailing list that interests you, you can subscribe direct from www.liszt.com or e-mail the mailing list itself.

[8] www.poynter.org/car/cg_carlists.htm

You can find a clear explanation of how to subscribe to listservs, plus a useful list of journalism related mailing lists, in McGuire, Stilborne, McAdams and Hyatt (2000).[9]

Finally, you should be warned that mailing lists can generate a great deal of traffic. Subscribers can receive scores of e-mails a day. You soon start a 'read' and 'unread' folder. Then you realize the 'unread' folder has four hundred messages in it, so you delete it and start again.

Check your mailing lists daily. Learn to scan messages and recognize the pre-occupations of frequent contributors. Be ruthless with the delete key and if your list offers a digest of all the messages of the day, try that.

Newsgroups

Newsgroups are another online meeting place but are very different in nature to mailing lists. If the mailing list is the private club, the newsgroup is the bar at the corner of the street. Unlike mailing lists, you normally do not have to subscribe to newsgroups. This makes access easier, which is usually through your Internet service provider where you can find enormous lists of newsgroups. Another place to look for newsgroups is at the old www.dejanews.com which has now been taken over by Google (Groups.Google.com). Here you can search for newsgroups or even individual discussion threads (lists of messages that have been posted in response to other messages). The other major difference to mailing lists is that newsgroups operate on an open platform. Anyone can read any message you post on a newsgroup board.

This has advantages and disadvantages. The good news is that there are newsgroups for virtually every subject under the sun. They also attract a younger user group than many mailing lists and so are good for topics such as music and other pop culture. Unfortunately, however, much of the material posted on newsgroups is chit-chat and of no value to you whatsoever as a journalist. But their spread of topics is so enormous, you can sometimes find more weighty material there.

[9] At pp. 109–111.

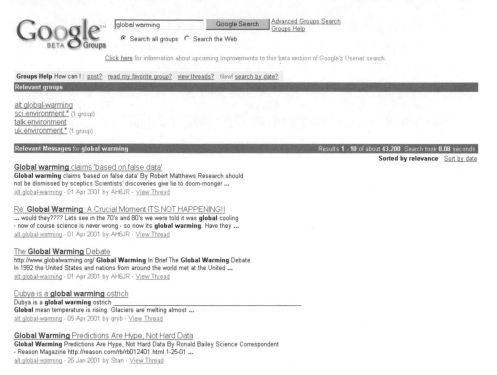

Figure 3.7: Imagine being able to join in any bar-room discussion of your choice. Welcome to the world of newsgroups. You can search for them on the new Google version of www.dejanews.com. (Google Brand Features are trademarks of Google, Inc.)

In practice, newsgroups tend to work better as a place to take the temperature, rather than contact experts or specialists. If you do spot someone who might be a good contact, you can always e-mail him or her directly, rather than giving the world your message.

Further reading and references

Houston, B. (1999). *CAR – A Practical Guide*. Bedford/St Martins.

Reddick, R. and King, E. (1997). *The Online Journalist*. 2nd edition.

McGuire, M., Stilborne, L., McAdams, M. and Hyatt, L. (2000). *The Internet Handbook for Researchers, Writers and Journalists*. Guildford Press.

Paul, N. (1999). *Computer-Assisted Research*, 4th edition. Bonus Books.

CAR guides and reference:

- www.groups.google.com/googlegroups/deja_announce-ment.html – the former dejanews, now taken over by Google. The best way to find newsgroups on the Net. If you cannot handle the URL, try www.dejanews.com and you will be diverted to the new service.
- www.jouralismnet.com – size, as they say, is not everything. However, the inestimable Julian Sher's sumptuous collection of links and tips for journalists is as good a place as any to start.
- www.liszt.com – the essential directory of discussion groups based on e-mails.
- http://powerreporting.com – a wealth of guidance on online research techniques.
- www.rawlinson.co.uk/CARpark_UK/ – a very useful collection of computer-assisted reporting and research resources for journalism in the UK.
- www.robertniles.com – consists of statistics skills every journalist should know.
- www.ryerson.ca/journal/mega11.htm – Dean Tudor's extensive CAR links from the Ryerson Institute for Computer Assisted Reporting in Canada.
- www.searchenginewatch – Danny Sullivan's essential guide to online search techniques.

General reference:

- www.bartleby.com/62/ – Roget's Thesaurus.
- www.britannica.com – an online version of the world-famous Encyclopedia Britannica.
- www.cc.columbia.edu/acis/bartleby/bartlett/ – Bartlett's Familiar Quotations, searchable.
- www.countrywatch.com – key data on nearly two hundred countries, as well as information on recent news stories.
- www.encarta.msn.com – Encarta encyclopedia.
- www.fowlerlibrary.com/kiosk/ – a factfile for every country of the world, with news and current events, history and culture, government and politics, economy and development.

- www.insanityideas.com/quotemachine/ – a database of quotations searchable by keyword, subject or author, as well as by category (e.g. insults).
- www.lifestyle.co.uk – a UK directory of links under categories such as money, community, news, health, computing, travel and women.
- www.peterwilkinson.karoo.net – topical quotations from people in the news, with an archive dating back to 1 January 2000.
- www.phon.uci.ac.uk/home/dave/TOC_H/Charities/ – an A–Z list of charities.
- www.ukbusinesspark.co.uk/bpmedi.htm – a day-by-day stream of brief news messages on the media industry, plus the latest company results and top company rankings.
- www.ukindex.co.uk – an index of UK Internet sites.
- www.worldemail.com – the world e-mail directory.
- http://w1.xrefer.com – definitions, synonyms and details of usage for words or phrases from a wide range of encyclopedias, dictionaries, thesauri, books of quotations, etc.

Political resources:

- www.cia.gov – the CIA's site.
- www.coi.gov.uk – news and information on government departments and agencies from the UK government's Central Office of Information.
- http://europa.eu.int/comm/index.htm – a directory of the European Commission's work programme, with a users' guide to accessing documents.
- www.oecd.org – site of the Organization for Economic Cooperation and Development. Activities, with news and events.
- www.official-documents.co.uk – official documents of the UK, published by the Stationery Office, House of Commons and House of Lords.
- www.ons.gov.uk – the site of the UK Office for National Statistics.
- www.open.gov.uk – a major resource of UK government information with a useful information locator facility.

- www.oultwood.com/localgov/ – links to local government web resources in the UK, Eire, Canada, Australia, New Zealand and South Africa.
- www.parliament.the-stationery-office.co.uk/pa/cm200001/ cmregmem/memi02.htm – the register of interests for Members of the UK Parliament.
- www.parliament.uk – site of the UK Houses of Parliament.
- www.politicalresources.net – international links.
- www.psr.keele.ac.uk – political science resources.
- www.trytel.com/~aberdeen/ – a directory of the politicians of the world, with addresses, lobbyist tools, etc.
- www.un.org – the site of the United Nations.
- www.whitehouse.gov – yes, that White House.

4 Writing

"The full stop is a great help to sanity."

Harold Evans, Essential English for Journalists[1]

Words are the worker bees of the Web and the Internet, used for basic text, headlines, captions, summaries, raw data, archived documents and millions of messages in newsgroups, listservs and e-mail. It is also the written word that makes the web itself work, through the linking of pages with Hyper *Text* Markup Language or HTML.

And yet, as we will see, the computer screen is not the easiest place to read large amounts of text. In particular, it has almost become a platitude that 'users won't scroll' down the screen to read a long story.

Not everyone agrees. Brock N. Meakes is Chief Washington Correspondent for MSNBC. He believes 'If you're a good writer and you have a good story to tell, people will read all the way through to the end, whether it's on the Web, in a newspaper or written on the ceiling of your hotel room. They will scroll if you write well.'[2]

---

[1] Evans (2000), p 19.
[2] Interview with author, June 2000.

You can write anything well or badly, except perhaps a list of data on a spreadsheet (although those nine words have probably just offended numerous CAR purists – powerful things, words, aren't they?).

No matter how you approach content provision, you will almost certainly use links, headlines and summaries. These are archetypal examples of the journalist as craftsman, as wordsmith. The skill that hones the headline has been passed down through generations of print journalists. But it's never been more relevant. The Web is home to a million headlines and a billion links. We need to get them right.

The Poynter Institute Eye Track Study of web viewing habits, published in 2000, suggests that online readers go to headlines, captions and story briefs first, rather than graphics and pictures. They use them as entry points to explore other pages. They will often read the full text of the stories, even returning to a page to do so. And, despite the accepted wisdom, they will scroll to read the whole piece if their interest is held. Good writing, as Meakes states, plays a key part in this.

So words and writing matter very much in the online world. That is why we are devoting this chapter to core writing skills, the kind you need in any medium. There are also writing techniques specifically for online. We will address these in Chapter 5 when we explore non-linear storytelling.

Core writing skills

The purpose of this book is to bring together the key principles and skills of online journalism and then tell you the best sources of further guidance.

It is no accident that the two best sources on core writing skills for online journalists are both long-established primers for newspaper journalists. Harold Evans' *Newsman's English* (now re-published as *Essential English for Journalists, Editors and Writers*) and William Strunk Jr's *The Elements of Style* (later revised by E. B. White) have provided wise counsel to generations of journalists.

Both urge economy of language, partly because space is limited for newspaper journalists. In contrast, pagination can be unlimited online. But Evans' rule of seeking 'the marriage of economy and accuracy' (2000) is also sound advice for the online journalist. Jakob Nielsen (2000) cites research that indicates reading from computer screens is about 25% slower than reading from paper. He recommends you should write 50% less text to accommodate this disadvantage and the discomfort caused by reading from screens (although screen resolution will improve in the next few years). This gives a fresh resonance to Evans' (2000) warning to newspaper journalists that 'nothing is so tiring to the reader as excavating nuggets of meaning from mountains of words'.

What follows includes, among other advice, a précis of some of the key points from both Evans and Strunk. Both of these seminal texts should be read in full, if you are serious about your writing.

Words and sentences

The first step to effective writing is widespread, critical reading. You should read many different newspapers. In the UK, the tabloids are sniffed at by some of the more 'serious-minded' journalists. But they contain many of the best examples of simple, effective writing. Read magazines, books and online sources. Read literature as well as factual material. Look for distinctive voices among the newspaper columnists and writers and study their work. You will not find any discernible style that has been imposed on their writing. Rather they will have a keen eye, quick wit and a sharp intellect, married to a clear understanding and respect for the power of simple language.

As journalists, sentences and words are the basic units of our currency and we must not devalue them. As Evans (2000) put it, 'Nothing so distinguishes good writing as vivid economy'. The following are guiding principles on the use of sentences and words when writing. They are not unbreakable rules, but you must have a good reason for not enforcing them. Most importantly, you must have thought carefully about those reasons and therefore also about your writing.

Sentences

You should always try to write directly. The basic structure of subject, verb and then object is a sound model. So, *the boy caught the ball*, not *the ball was caught by the boy.* ·

Sentences that start with a subordinate clause can be another example of indirect writing. *After I have finished this cup of tea, I will go into the garden* is self-evidently less direct than *I will go into the garden after I have finished this cup of tea.* If you find yourself starting a sentence with 'after', 'during', 'although', etc., stop and consider whether that is the best structure.

Keep your sentences short and to the point. You can start your sentence well, with the main clause, but still find it trailing off in a clutter of subordinate clauses. These will need re-writing as shorter sentences.

As Leslie Sellers remarks in his invaluable text, *The Simple Subs Book* (1968)[3]:

> '. . . over-long sentences are death to readability. They are usually of involved construction, and involved sentences have to be read twice to get their full meaning . . . Nothing that can't be absorbed at first reading ought to appear in a newspaper. Yet night after night and week after week these jigsaw puzzles get into print.'

A good rule to avoid convoluted sentences is to limit each to communicating one basic thought or piece of information.

But avoid making *all* your sentences short and snappy. This can produce an unpleasant staccato, machine-gun effect that is wearing for the reader. A mix of sentence lengths can improve the rhythm of your writing. It also accentuates the dramatic impact of short sentences when you use them for that reason.

Do not be afraid of breaking the basic rules of grammar if it enhances the effectiveness of your message. Journalists write

---

[3] Harold Evans' book *Newsman's English* languished out of print for many years until a campaign was waged successfully by journalists and those teaching journalism to get a new edition published. I often think a similar movement should be launched to bring Seller's book back into public circulation, for the benefit of young journalists and students.

sentences without verbs, start sentences with conjunctions ('but', 'and', etc.) and end them with prepositions ('of', 'for', etc.). This is the syntax of their readers and makes the journalist's message more acceptable and easily understood. Again, such approaches (especially the non-verb sentence) should not be over-used but they are perfectly legitimate techniques.

Try to write actively, about things happening to people rather than not happening. So a football team might *escape relegation*, rather than *not be relegated*.

Use punctuation correctly. Commas should be used where there is a mental pause in the sentence. A sentence can be confusing or even misleading without them. But use too many, and your sentence coughs and splutters along the page, making little headway. If you're using a lot of commas, this again may suggest that your sentence needs splitting into several smaller ones. Apostrophes and their positioning are another blind spot for many aspiring journalists. The office belonging to your singular client is your client**'s** office. The office belonging to your plural client**s** is your client**s'** office. But there is one very important anomaly to remember – *it's* means *it is* and not 'belonging to it'. Please.

Finally, constantly work and rework your piece, within your time limits, to improve the sense and flow of your writing. This should be an enjoyable challenge, not a chore. Even if it is the latter, as Sellers observes, 'struggle is good for the soul.'

Words

As Keith Waterhouse (1989) remarks 'Every word that gets into print should have something to say'. So:

- don't use more words than you need;
- avoid long words if shorter alternatives are available;
- avoid words with complex meanings if simpler alternatives are available;
- use words with a concrete, rather than an abstract, meaning whenever possible;
- be specific rather than use generalities;
- give words their correct meaning.

In addition to these guidelines, you should also be aware of some of the elephant traps awaiting the inexperienced journalist. Here are a few of the deepest.

The frequent use of adjectives or adverbs to 'pump a story up' often has the opposite effect. As Waterhouse puts it: 'Smothering an intro in a ketchup of adjectives does little to improve its flavour'. Expressing the facts of the story clearly and vigourously should provide all the necessary impact. If you have to prop up a story with adjectives, question whether it's worth writing in the first place.

Avoid an excessive use of clichés. They can be trite and tired. That isn't to say clichés should be avoided like the plague. As Sellers explains: 'Cliché chopping ought not to get out of hand. In many cases the cliché is the warm familiar phrase that the readers recognise, that puts things in a nutshell.'

Avoid tautologies whenever possible. General consensus or mutual agreement (how can you have any other?), strange phenomena (presumably to distinguish it from the mundane variety) and continue to remain (as opposed to stopping to remain?) are just three examples of words that have been wedded in unholy matrimony by constant, unthinking usage. You don't need to say something twice to get the message across.

You should filter out all jargon and 'officialese'. This shouldn't be difficult for the journalist who has to discover what the jargon means in simple terms anyway, to understand the story. Once he or she has a 'plain language' explanation, it would seem obvious to use it in their written account. Instead, too many journalists inexplicably retreat back into the dark world of jargon when finally writing their story. How do they expect their readers to understand the same dead, grey language that confounded them, the journalists, in the first place?

This mistake is usually made because the journalist is either under pressure or lazy. It is easier for them to pass on the official gobbledegook to readers than exert the necessary effort to explain it in simple terms. Occasionally, and more worryingly, it can also occur because the journalist doesn't understand the jargon and so can only repeat it rather than interpret it. That is a cardinal sin.

As I said at the beginning of this book, online journalism is a broad church and includes those who provide content for their own organizations, such as companies, local authorities and charities. These people find it particularly difficult to avoid jargon because they don't always spot it. Jargon is the verbal and written shorthand of the workplace. It can be useful in that context, but jargon has the reverse effect when used in external communication. It excludes readers, who may also be clients and customers. The trouble is, jargon becomes so engrained within an organization that its use becomes subconscious. One solution is to employ some jargon-busters to periodically test such sites, laypeople who know little about the organizations in question.

Finally, use quotes appropriately. Do not use a direct quote to impart mundane information. You can summarize that more effectively in your general text. When possible, use quotes to convey emotion, feeling, drama or information that is pivotal to the story development.

The difficulty with giving guidelines on writing words and sentences is just that . . . they are guidelines: a set of do's and don'ts that may sound admirable but don't spur people into action. I have never met a journalism student who would challenge the Evans or Strunk doctrine. But that doesn't mean they practice it. Examples are usually more persuasive than rules and who better to provide an example than Harold Evans himself.

Evans (2000) is very quotable because he writes so well. There are many lines I could have chosen. But for this example, let's look at a single sentence, quoted earlier in this chapter: 'Nothing so distinguishes good writing as vivid economy'.

Now Evans may not have given this sentence much thought when he wrote it. He might find it laughable to see it now subject to such scrutiny. I am certainly not suggesting it is the finest example of his *oeuvre*. But it will suffice for this exercise, particularly as it is a single idea encapsulated in a single sentence – the essence, some might say, of journalism. I could have picked a score like it from Evans' book *Essential English for Journalists, Editors and Writers*. So it's also typical.

There are three reasons why this sentence is an example of good writing:

- the idea that it communicates is, clear and apposite;
- the language used is simple and direct. But within that short sentence Evans also includes the juxtaposition of two apparent opposites in 'vivid' and 'economy'. The effect is both arresting and thought provoking;
- put those two qualities together – the direct simplicity of both message and language with the striking phrase at the end – and the sentence, and this is the beauty of it, does exactly what it says.

Evans' sentence may seem unremarkable but, in less skilful hands, the sentiment it expressed could have degenerated too easily into cliché. "Keep it tight and bright" might approximately mean the same thing but it doesn't begin to *say* the same thing. And that makes all the difference.

Story structure

The correct use of words and sentences enhances all written communication. But what about news in particular? How do you harness these core writing skills to the additional requirement to summarize an often complex set of events or information in a direct style and limited space?

Two things fill a journalist's mind when they are writing – ideas and language. Language, as we've seen, is critically important and shapes the structure of the sentence and the paragraph. But ideas shape the structure of the story. And story structure is fundamental to your readers' understanding of your message.

As David Randall (1999) explains, in his book *The Universal Journalist*:

'The most important part of writing is what happens inside your head between finishing your research and putting the first word down. You have got to think about your material and decide what it is about and what you want to do with it.

Composition is not merely the business of arranging words, it is the business of organising thought. It does not matter how wonderful you are at conjuring up colourful phrases or witty remarks, if you have not got a clear idea of what you want to say it will show.'

In traditional news writing, the structure of the story, in particular the introduction or lead, can be heavily influenced by the imperative of delivering maximum news value to your readers quickly. This is particularly true in action or event driven stories such as incidents of crime or accidents. Journalists often say these stories 'write themselves', reducing the need for original approaches or perspectives from the reporter. 'Ideas' here can mean simply the skilful distillation of essential information infused with a zest of fine observational detail.

However, issue or information driven stories are a different matter. Here the journalist is expected to explain and interpret and much of this comes from the careful structuring of the introduction and the rest of the story.

So, as journalists we write with ideas on how to convey our message, be it factual information or human emotion. But we do also write with words. You can structure your story with absolute clarity but then cloud your readers' understanding with dismal language.

You need both clear structure and the right words; and when ideas and language come together effectively, the journalist finds their 'voice', their distinctive view and its expression.

Story construction is the preoccupation of most writers. But in journalism it has a particular importance. Reporters have to juggle three essentials when writing their stories:

- identifying the elements of the story that will be of greatest interest to their readers;
- structuring the story in a way that will deliver these elements as effectively as possible;
- presenting them in a way that will make maximum use of the medium they are working within and engage the maximum number of readers for the maximum length of time.

In newspapers and broadcasting this usually means producing a single story with a carefully constructed beginning, middle and end. This is a linear construction. The beginning leads to the middle, which leads to the end. The story is written or recorded to be consumed in that order. If you break that relationship, for example by starting to read, view or hear the piece halfway through, you cannot expect to understand fully what then follows.

Before we look at online story construction in detail, let's just familiarize ourselves with the best known and most widely accepted model for traditional linear news story construction. As we will soon see, it might still have its uses.

Yes, the pyramid

Anyone familiar with journalism textbooks will know all about pyramid structure, used for news stories in newspapers and broadcasting. Quite simply the essence of a story should be placed at the top of the pyramid, with further development and amplification of the main points below, before finally tapering out to a base of background material.

Some people use the model of an 'inverted pyramid' – a pyramid standing on its head. Along with Wynford Hicks (1999), I can't understand the reason for this. The model works far better in the normal upright position with the wide base at the bottom. In that way the pyramid shape, from the top down, reflects both the importance and the *amount* that will be written. In the inverted position, it only reflects the importance (the biggest section being at the top). Please do not write introductions that are fifteen times bigger than the background material at the end of the story.

The pyramid shape offers two benefits. First, the reader can get the essence of the story by reading just the introduction. Second, newspaper sub-editors, pressed for space and time, can cut pyramid shaped stories from the bottom up and not destroy their sense.

Intros

So, what goes into the apex of the pyramid, or to use a more modern analogy, the nose cone of the rocket? The all-important intro, that's what. The first paragraphs. These are the most common cause of stress and anguish in young journalists who have to write them and older sub-editors who have to read them (and rewrite them).

Writing good intros is not easy. As Waterhouse (1989) points out: 'The first paragraph has to contain the essence of the story in perhaps 25 words.' Then, just like our pyramid, the story gradually fans out, using the same principle to expand on the essence in the next three or four paragraphs.

What goes into those initial paragraphs takes on added importance when writing for online. People often scan stories on web pages. They want to get to the point quickly. Also, stories can be 'top-sliced' (using the first few paragraphs) for distribution to mobile phones and personal organizers. To assist this, BBC News Online have their '4 par rule'. *The Online Journalist* (2000) is the BBC's handbook for their News Online journalists. It states that as much vital information as possible should go into the first four paragraphs of a story, including context and background, This is to ensure that the story will make sense if the first four paragraphs are read in isolation. Also, each paragraph should have a clear purpose and simple structure. Journalists should limit themselves to one idea per paragraph.

This discipline becomes particularly important when you consider that journalists at BBC News Online are set a word limit of 400–500 words for main stories in their entirety (those in the top three of its index) and 250–350 words for other stories. Not much room for the unnecessary or the convoluted. As *The Online Journalist* explains:

> 'All stories should be written in a clear and accessible manner – we are writing for a general audience and a global one. We must not assume too much knowledge. The importance of the story – why we should care – needs to be flagged up early on, as should the impact on ordinary people. Spell it out every time!'

So the beginning of the story – the intro – is critically important. But how do you choose what goes in it?

Here we should cast our mind back to Chapter 2, when we analysed the triggers that made readers think something was newsworthy. Looking for relevance, revelation and arousal guided our 'gathering-in' of information. Writing a story is a continuation of that reporting process. Why should we forget these qualities when we choose what we 'send out' in our writing?

So, when constructing your intro, you should look for information that is new (revelation) to your reader and will also grab their interest through being unusual or dramatic (arousal). As Lord Nortchliffe put it, 'News is anything out of the ordinary'. But the relevance of the story to these readers must also be spelt out immediately. This is why reporters on local newspapers are always taught to get a geographical reference from their area into the first sentence of any story. It emphasizes the relevance of the story. Similarly a temporal reference (today, tomorrow, etc.) emphasizes that this news is happening within their community now, increasing its relevance and any revelation.

However, another imperative for the intro is that it should be short. There is always a tension between what you want to say and the space available. The more demands you make of the intro, the greater the likelihood that it will become distended and too complex. You have to think hard about the news triggers in your story, be ruthless in your selection but still attempt to hit as many of them as possible in your first 25 words. As Sellers (1968) puts it: 'Clarity, tightness, information – and the news point that is going to start people talking. These are the qualities to seek'.

Essentially, an intro places a number of signposts for the reader, indicating the information that will be clarified and amplified in the paragraphs that follow. And your choice of words is critically important, as an examination of even the most straightforward trigger, location reference, illustrates.

Imagine you are writing about plans to build a chemical works on the outskirts of 'Bloggstown', next to a popular public open space visited regularly by people from the town and surrounding villages. You want to include all these location reference points in your story because they will maximise its relevance to your readers. But put them all into the first sentence, and you will struggle to produce anything readable. So you restrict yourself to a single location reference in the first sentence. Then build from there, tightening the location focus in succeeding paragraphs.

The essence of your intro could be 'Firm to build chemical plant outside Bloggstown'. This immediately gets the attention of the people of Bloggstown. But it is not very specific. Whereabouts outside Bloggstown? The general nature of the location in the intro will potentially engage the interest of all people living outside the town – north, south, east and west. But beware of this catchall approach. You will have to be specific soon in the story and people whose interest/fears have been aroused, only to find the story has little relevance to them because they live on the other side of town, will jettison it in large numbers, feeling slightly duped.

How about 'Firm plan to build chemical plant next to Bloggstown beauty spot.' This is more specific (even if there is more than one local beauty spot, this can be explained in the next sentence). So it will definitely attract the geographical community living near the public open space in question.

But the simple addition of the words 'beauty spot' will also broaden the relevance of the story. It will engage another community, a community of interest – all those nature lovers who frequently travel from miles around to visit the beauty spot (and who may come from a wider geographical area, so broadening the location relevance beyond 'outside Bloggstown').

The additional words also create another news trigger – arousal. The juxtaposition of chemical plant and beauty spot adds an element of discord or even drama that increases the trigger value of the location relevance.

It may seem faintly ridiculous to consider the use of two words in such depth. But this is what the journalist must do, and hopefully enjoy. With practice, it will become almost an instinctive process. But the best journalists still constantly work and rework their writing, never satisfied with what they've produced. The aim is to make every word in an intro (and everywhere else in your piece) earn its corn. Each word is there by right. No passengers allowed. You should always try to reduce the words and yet maximize the news value whenever writing or editing your own text.

This means getting to the main thrust of the story immediately. Try to make the very first word a strong, specific one. Do not drown your readers in a murky soup of councils, committees, chairmen/women and departments. If these bodies have made a significant decision (not always the case), tell the reader what it is and what effect it will have on them. The fine detail of which body made the decision can come after the first couple of paras.

Also, avoid starting an intro with direct quotes. People don't know who's uttering them. Avoid introducing unidentified facts, events or people at the very start of a story as it can confuse the reader. Confusion rapidly leads to disinterest and then disengagement, particularly in the scanning online environment.

The BBC is aware of this precarious grip on the attention of the online reader and makes an interesting comparison with broadcasting: 'On radio and TV, you sometimes have to lead listeners/viewers gently into a story. On the Web, you need to get into the story immediately' (*The Online Journalist*, 2000).

This is why some other newspaper intro techniques are less successful for online. The most well known is probably the delayed drop. This is where the main thrust of the story, it's *raison d'être* so to speak, is not in the first paragraph. Instead it is placed later in the story, the readers usually being gently led towards it by a narrative style of writing.

As Sellers (1968) points out, even in newspapers the delayed drop can pose problems:

> This form of intro – the delayed drop, the slow burn – is the most difficult one to practise. It assumes that the story is so beautifully written, so compulsively readable, that the customer will be swept along till he reaches a buried news point 12 paragraphs on.

> But life is not like that. The average newspaper reader does not approach his paper as he does a short story: it is quite likely that he is reading it standing in a bus or in the four and half minutes he is waiting for a train. The incidental facts are probably not vivid enough to carry him through to a climax . . . All this is not to say that delayed drop stories are out. But 99 times out of a hundred the news is the thing.

The delayed drop is a particularly brave opening gambit for the online writer, given that online readers face many on-screen distractions and scan at a speed nearer Sonic the Hedgehog than a Sunday stroll.

Headlines

Harold Evans (2000) is in no doubt about the importance of headline writing: 'Writing good headlines is 50% of text editors' skills. Every bit of time chiselling out the right words in the right sequence is time well spent'.

Evans' chisel becomes a very blunt instrument in the hands of many online writers and editors. Headlines are used with little apparent thought for either their purpose or appearance. This is a particularly perverse practice within the online medium, given the reading habits of users highlighted by the Poynter Institute Eye Track study mentioned earlier. As Evans (2000) explains, the headline serves two main purposes: first, to attract as many readers as possible into the text of the story. Second, for those who do not read further, headlines can still have an effect, 'for many who do not read the story none the less retain an impression from *scanning* the headline.' (author's italics).

The headline carries an additional responsibility within online journalism. It provides important guidance and context for those readers who access individual sections of stories on their own, separated from the rest of the coverage (for example if linked to a section direct from another site or a search engine). The BBC are aware of this:

'Our headlines – particularly those on the Global, UK and World indexes – are increasingly being extracted and being sent elsewhere to the BBC ticker and the BBC Homepage, mobile phones, etc. They also appear in Related Stories. So while more cryptic headlines can appear fine accompanied by the summary, they can be nonsense standing alone. It is therefore essential that they bear some direct relationship to the story. They can be clever and enticing but please make them intelligible out of context of the story' (*The Online Journalist*, 2000).

Leslie Sellers (1968) offers a number of basic rules that every headline writer would do well to remember:

- use the active voice and the present tense whenever possible ('MPs urge Blair to act' rather than 'Call for action from MPs';
- avoid punctuation (e.g. commas and apostrophes) in headlines; as Sellers remarks 'a comma means a two-part headline which is slower';
- avoid the anonymous he, she or they; specify occupation, age, etc. and personalize whenever appropriate (Bush instead of US President);
- avoid cramming in too much information;
- in the case of a double-line heading, try to make the first line make sense on its own because it represents a complete thought on its own.

Sellers also warns against the over-use of headline jargon. He believes words such as 'bid', 'slash' and 'rapped' are okay because they're short and make the point quickly but

there is a danger here. Words such as quit, probe, rush, cut, ban, dash, slash, crash, quiz and hits are so useful that they tend to be overworked. They become part of the lazy sub's armoury. Instead of being kept for the occasion when no other word will do the job, they are used out of habit, so that the paper is filled to overflowing with them.

Some online publishers would object to the use of any of these words, ever. The BBC advise against what they call 'jargon and clichés' such as 'slammed' and 'blasted' and "screamers" (use of exclamation marks). The use of such headline language is very much down to the individual house style of news operations and, as Sellers points out, the imagination, or lack of it, of the sub-editor.

Another important consideration is the spread of your readership. Sellers advises against specific place names in headlines unless they have a specific purpose. This is a particular danger for online journalists, given the global readership of sites. Specific geographic references that might convey meaning to a domestic readership (e.g. Leighton Buzzard) could puzzle and so discourage a worldwide readership. This challenge extends to all areas of headline writing, not just place names. For example, during the outbreak of foot and mouth disease among livestock in the UK in 2001, it was noticeable that BBC News usually referred to it as 'Farm disease' in its headlines, presumably because some countries would not be familiar with the term 'foot and mouth' (it's also shorter).

The final point to be made about writing headlines is aimed at those people who write headlines for others. No matter how pressurized you are, it's vitally important that you both read and understand the whole story submitted to you. You must read everything because the main news point might not be in the first paragraph. And you must understand both the story and its importance to your readership. You cannot make judgements about the content of a headline if you do not understand the background to the story. As Evans states, you should 'think hard on what single element of the story it is which makes it new, different and worth its space in the paper' . . . or the website. He continues 'The art of the headline lies in imagination and vocabulary; the craft lies in accuracy of content, attractiveness of appearance and practicality'. Not something to be thrown together at the last moment.

Captions, summaries and links

Captions for pictures can also be an afterthought, which is a mistake. The most common fault with captions is to make them too descriptive. Just as a television journalist is taught to let pictures tell their own story and be sparing with the voice-over, so a caption writer must not waste their limited space (usually one line) simply describing what the reader can see in the picture anyway. As Sellers (1968) points out 'Writing an accompaniment for a picture is an entirely different art, in which the picture is the intro, the attention-catcher, and the rest can fall more gently into place'.

So a caption should not just describe what you can already see or state the obvious. Often you do need to impart basic information, for example someone's name, to identify that person's picture from the other half a dozen names in the story. But you will usually want to add other details explaining the person's relevance to the story. Remember, people may read a caption before the main text of a story.

Fitting two separate pieces of information into one line is not easy. One common technique among caption writers is to use a colon to establish a link between the two pieces of information. This can work in either order. So a story about the craze of Digimon toys sweeping the UK might have a picture of one of them with the caption: 'Digimon: sweeping the nation' or 'Latest craze: Digimon toys'.

Summaries are also used extensively on online news sites, outlining the story and hopefully inviting the reader to click through to the detailed coverage. Again these need to be written carefully. They should not necessarily be the first two paragraphs of the story and they certainly should not repeat what is in the headline as this will accompany them on the page. The BBC limit their summaries to one sentence in the present tense.

There is one area where online provides a new challenge for the journalist as text editor and that is in the labelling of links. How often have you seen a site inviting you to link to other pages or sites without giving you any clear idea of what to expect or why you should go there? Internal links (linking you to other pages within your own site) are often the most challenging. The external link can be summarized by using the name of the organization that you are linking to. But internal links might take you to pages containing quite complex content, such as 'Related Stories'. You must think carefully how to summarize these in a way that makes sense to your user. A good check on this is to periodically show your links to someone unfamiliar with the previous coverage and see if they can understand them.

So, structure and writing, ideas and language – essential determinants of how you select and present your information. It's not hard to see how the simplicity of classic news writing will benefit online journalism. But what is the appropriate story *construction* for this medium? That's what we turn our attention to next.

Further reading and references

BBC (2000). *The Online Journalist*, V. 2.06, April 2000.

Evans, H. (2000*). Essential English for Journalists, Editors and Writers*. Pimlico.

Hicks, W. (1998). *English for Journalists*, 2nd edition. Routledge.

Hicks, W. (1999*). Writing for Journalists*. Routledge.

Keeble, R. (1998). *The Newspapers Handbook*, second edition. Routledge.

Nielsen, J. (2000). *Designing Web Usability*. New Riders.

The Poynter Institute (2000). Eye Track Study.

Randall, D. (1999). *The Universal Journalist*. Pluto Press.

Sellers, L. (1968).*The Simple Subs book* (out of print).

Strunk, W. Jr (1979) *The Elements of Style,* 3rd edition (revised by E. White). Macmillan.

Waterhouse, K. (1989) *On Newspaper style*. Penguin.

Zinsser, W. (1998). *On Writing Well*, 6th edition. Harper Perennial.

■ www.contentious.com – Amy Gahran's valuable e-zine for online content creator and publishers.

■ www.content-exchange.com – a digital marketplace for online content creators and publishers. Includes the Content Spotlight e-mail newsletter.

■ www.ecomomist.com/editorial/freeforall/library/styleguide/ – online guide to help users write clearly and accurately from *The Economist* magazine.

■ www.planetarynews.com – Steve Outing's comprehensive site, including news, information and gateways to discussion lists on online news, online writing and online newspapers.

5 Online story construction

'The trick is not to take an analogue mind into a digital world.'

Jeanette Winterson, author[1]

Non-linear storytelling

Newspaper and broadcast stories, as was seen in Chapter 4, are built on a linear model. However, much has been written about the non-linear nature of online. Users have the power to go where they please, gathering content. They can link from information chunk to audio file, to database, to graphic, to text summary, to video, to archive, and then disappear through an external link to another site. That does not mean that all users do, but they can if they wish. This pattern of consuming information is a haphazard zig-zag rather than a line. And every pathway created by every user can be different.

Online is also, primarily, an on-screen environment.[2] Screens come in all shapes, sizes and locations, but they still have an inferior resolution to the high-quality printed page. Using screens can be hard work.

[1] Interview in *The Industry Standard*, p. 79. November 2000.
[2] Primarily, but not always. Audio can be accessed on line and, of course, there are the millions of hard copies of web pages printed off every day.

Put these two factors together – the commitment needed for a reader to stay and the freedom they have to roam – and you can see that online journalists and content providers must think long and hard about how they construct and present their stories. It is a very different environment from the 'old' media of newspapers, radio and television.

In the mid-1990s it became apparent that a new approach to online story construction was being adopted. One of the leading voices to emerge was that of Leah Gentry, who, first at the Orange County Register and Chicago Tribune and later at latimes.com, espoused an approach to 'non-linear storytelling' which many since have followed.

As Gentry herself puts it:

The fundamental theory behind non-linear storytelling for the web is that you need to look at the medium you're working in and ask 'What are the strengths of this medium and how can I use those strengths to help me tell my story?'. So you work with the medium instead of against the medium.[3]

It is striking how frequently Gentry's initial guidelines, which date back to 1996, are still endorsed and re-stated by online journalists and content providers. They have stood the test of turbulent times and so bear repeating here, in a slightly abridged form.

- Rule 1 – follow the guidelines of good journalism. The traditional methods of careful and unbiased reporting, using compelling writing, photography, audio and video, will translate well into the new media.
- Rule 2 – 'leverage the strengths of the medium'. This phrase has rung in my ears since I first heard Leah Gentry talk about it at a conference in 1997. She defines the strengths as linking, immediacy, interactivity, multimedia and depth. These, especially when combined, are what make online journalism distinctive.

[3] Interview with author, July 2000.

- Rules 3 and 4 – deconstruct, reconstruct and storyboard. Divide your story into component pieces, look for similarities or trends in those pieces, group your pieces into logical categories, reconstruct your story, using storyboards, to group the pieces under those categories and build cross-links. Each story will have one section which is the 'linear kernel' – the essence of the story – plus other sections which will provide additional information, background and explanations.
- Rule 5 – do not use technology out of context. Anything that does not further a story is visual noise.[4]

The traditional pyramid structure, as we have seen, positions the introduction, development and background of a story within one solid block of interlocking sections. This method produces lengthy single pieces, carefully developed and structured. This can be an advantage in newspapers, helping to orientate readers through the story. However, such a treatment presented problems for online from the outset.

Gentry's approach, adopted at least in theory by many in the online content community, was to break up the monolith by dismantling the pyramid.

The reason for this, as explained in Chapter 4, is that it takes longer and is more tiring (requiring scrolling) to read from a screen than a printed page. Of course, larger single stories also mean bigger files which take longer to download. Separating your story into different sections you will ameliorate these problems. If you are not careful, however, you might create a few others, for example causing the reader confusion when navigating your sections. However, it should certainly make it easier for readers to download and to scan rather than scroll.

This improvement in usability might be reason enough to follow the Gentry model. But there are two other factors, more fundamental to your journalism, that help to explain why the 'deconstruction–reconstruction' approach has been central to the development of online journalism during the formative years.

[4] www.naa.org

- ■ 'Chunking' your story maximizes the potential readership. Stories can be complex, with various themes, angles and areas of coverage. As a result, readers will engage with different parts of the story and for different reasons. When presented with a single pyramid story, readers have to work through the stuff that doesn't engage them to find the material that does. Some do not bother and move on. This minimizes the potential readership. But if the story is segmented into different sections, which the reader can spot from a distance (via a search engine) and read separately, without having to refer to the other sections, you can fulfil the potential of the user-driven medium and maximize the potential readership.

- ■ Separating the story into chunks also increases the number of entry points for the distinctive elements of online. When Leah Gentry urged us all to 'leverage the strengths of the medium', she wanted us to work with and not against the online medium. Breaking your story into sections allows you to introduce bespoke multimedia, interactivity and linkage as constituent elements of each section. If the online story is a single pyramid, most of these elements (which are fundamental rather than value added) are made peripheral rather than integral. By delivering the story in different sections, you provide multiple entry points for these important journalistic tools.

So chunking makes sense. Surely then, there's no place for the traditional pyramid structure within the segmented world of online writing and content creation? Well there is, actually. But to understand why, we first have to take a step back.

A place for linearity?

We are repeatedly told that online is a non-linear medium, but what does that mean? Is anything truly non-linear? An Ornette Coleman solo, perhaps, but that's another matter.

Is it not more accurate to say that online applications such as surfing the web involve the non-linear *consumption* of mainly *linear* products? Leah Gentry talks of the linear kernel, but text chunks, story summaries, and audio and video files are all built individually on a linear pattern. As a consumption model, online is completely irregular and unpredictable. However, as a production model, it is a paragon of linearity, at least at the level of the 'info chunk'. Journalism and content creation need production models. For text, there is not much to beat the pyramid for linearity.

So when we dismantle the pyramid for online use, do we take it apart from the apex down, in three or four sections like a child's wooden block toy? This would leave us with some very strange shapes, and therefore story structures. Surely, instead, we build a series of linked pyramid-shaped chunks, which means we do not discard it completely.

Before moving on, we should consider three other reasons for retaining a linear structure when writing for online.

First, some people want news at any time. They seek a similar linear product to the 'old media' when they go online. They use this medium primarily because of its immediacy, rather than its ability to break a story down into different chunks. They are seeking a concise digest of a story or the news in general, but they want it now, even at three o'clock in the morning, and they want it fresh. Not that it always comes that way.

Second, some people want news in any place. Wireless Internet delivers news and information to your mobile phone. However, the clumsy interface (small screen size and restricted command input) discourages a 'rich media' experience. At the moment, it's better to keep it straight and simple. Keep it linear.

Finally, a short fanfare on muted trumpet for shovelware. This is usually a term of abuse among the cognoscenti, referring to the way newspapers put their hard copy content direct online with little or no adaptation for the new medium. The complete pyramid in all its digital glory.

However, actually, some people rather like shovelware. The global reach of the web allows citizens in exile who are unable to buy their local paper on the other side of the world to pick up a copy online. They want the back page sports reports exactly as they appear in the printed version – the same style, the same content . . . the same linear structure. Long live linearity.

Once again, the medium is telling the journalist to be flexible, not dogmatic and that it's the user who decides. In online journalism there is a role for both the deconstructed and the digest.

How to separate a story into chunks

Linearity is central to how we build each chunk, but how do we decide what each chunk should be? Should there be any criteria for how we segment our stories?

Segmentation can be influenced by:

- the characteristics of the story;
- the needs and interests of the user; and
- the delivery platform being used.

The 'characteristics of the story' refers to the way the story itself can influence how you segment it in the following three ways.

- The scale and duration of coverage – is this a major breaking story which could require many separate pages and constant updates?
- The breadth and depth of coverage – is this a complex story with many different facets and, thus, many different potential readerships?
- The range of coverage – does this story lend itself to multimedia, interactive features, etc.?

Now this is hardly rocket science, but it teaches us to take every story on its merits and give it the appropriate treatment. The story should drive the segmentation process, rather than dogma, habit or automated systems.

The second influence on story segmentation, not surprisingly, is the user. When deconstructing and reconstructing, you need to consider the following.

- The user's interests – which parts of the story's subject-matter will appeal to your target user groups?
- The user's needs – does he or she want constant updates, detailed breakdown and explanation, personalized interactive features, raw data, print-offs, etc.?

The final factor is the available delivery platform. Delivering the same story to multiple platforms (e.g. PCs, mobile phones and web television) will become more commonplace because it makes economic sense. News is an expensive commodity to generate, so you should get it out to as many people in as many forms as possible. However, the same story will need different constructions to make it function effectively on different platforms.

So, let's recap. We've seen that chunking is usually (but not always) the best way to construct a story or information for online consumption. We've also looked at criteria that guide the chunking process. But how do we construct the individual chunks? The answer is by using clean and direct writing. We may also apply a pyramid construction to give our chunks a scannable lead to summarize the content. But are there any other writing or story construction techniques that specifically suit online? Here are several to consider.

Make sure each individual chunk can 'stand alone'. People may arrive at a section of your story from another site, read it and then disappear to another corner of the Internet without touching the rest of your story. They should be able to read a single chunk in isolation and make sense of it. This means you have to provide editorial as well as navigational orientation and context for your reader. This is more difficult than it sounds because you must also accommodate the user who works through all the chunks of your story and does not want the same context again and again. It is a little like the television text writer who writes a story over several pages but doesn't know which page will be seen first by any single viewer. One writer is helping the reader with no control. The other is helping the reader to have total control. However, the requirement is the same.

Sometimes your copy must provide more than editorial context. It must also support inadequate site navigation. As Amy Gahran points out,[5] you can be hired to provide content for a site where the framework interface does not provide readers with enough context or orientation. Your content is going to sit in the middle of this mess. So, what do you do? She makes three suggestions:

---

[5] www.contentious.com

- mention your primary target audience in your lead or introduction;
- link to the site's home page early in the piece; and
- be explicit at the start of your piece about the area it will cover.

You must also grab the attention of the users – it is dangerous to stereotype web usage, but it is now accepted that a significant number of people scan web pages rather than read them in detail. However, there is still too often a perception gap between the providers and recipients of web content. As usability expert Steve Krug (2000) puts it, 'We're thinking "great literature" (or at least "product brochure") while the user's reality is much closer to "billboard going by at 60 miles an hour".'

Krug accepts that he is offering a simplistic view to make a fundamental point. He also points out that documents such as news stories or reports may hold the reader's attention for longer. However, he says, most people scan in a hurry, looking for words or phrases to catch their eye.

Krug's focus is on the design of sites. Design is an integral part of how you communicate, and we will come to in Chapter 7. For now, we will concentrate on the content. Can we write our stories in a way that will at least make the speeding motorist slow down and take a look?

Writing for online

Jakob Nielsen (1999) offers three rules for writing on the Web:

- be succinct – use no more than 50% of the text you would have written for the same story in print;
- write for scannability – use short paragraphs, subheadings and bulleted lists instead of long blocks of text; and
- use hypertext to split up long blocks of information into multiple pages.

Nielsen is also an advocate of plain language and pyramid structures.

Crawford Kilian[6] emphasizes the importance of 'hooking an impatient visitor . . . Your readers are skimming and scanning, so use both headlines and text to grab them.' His advice is:

- make headlines simple and informative;
- use quotation marks in text because people seem to prefer what someone actually said;
- include questions, as they make us seek the answer;
- include unusual statements, as readers love to be surprised;
- include the 'promise of conflict – we love fights';
- use news pegs 'to tie content to the coat-tails of some big current event'; and
- address the reader directly.

Jakob Nielsen emphasizes the value of web editors and Alysson Troffer[7] has some useful guidelines for editing 'non-sequential content' in the e-zine *Contentious*. As well as keeping chunks short and self-contained, she suggests editing them in random, rather than sequential, order. This helps to 'ensure a suitable and accessible organization for your readers'.

To accommodate scanning, she suggests that you:

- get right to the point;
- emphasize what is new or different about each chunk;
- avoid the 'as shown above' syndrome– you should not write your story as if all users will read all the chunks, but instead provide links and context on each page; and
- make pronoun references explicit and close – 'Whatever "it" refers to may have scrolled off your reader's screen.'

Like Nielsen and Kilian, Troffer also stresses the importance of plain language, particularly in headlines:

Your headings and page titles should explain clearly the topic addressed on each page in terms that reflect your audience's

[6] www.contentious.com
[7] www.contentious.com

perspective. Avoid cute, clever or cryptic headings, as well as headings that reflect only the author's perspective. Remember – when readers are scanning one of your pages, all they will really 'see' at first will be the page title and headings.

Making story chunks stand alone and scannable are two of the fundamentals of web writing. Yet is there room within this 'new' medium for more innovative approaches?

It is several years since Carole Rich[8] published her study into news writing for the web. In it, she acknowledged the value of the pyramid structure but also suggested experimentation:

> If writers are trying to entice reading, other styles must be explored. Experiments with writing on the Web involve many fiction sites, and fiction is not written in an inverted pyramid style. The Web offers a chance to be as eclectic in writing styles as it is in its reading population. One size does not fit all!

Janet Murray (1997), author of *Hamlet on the Holodeck*, talked of using segmentation to deliver an interlocking plot from different points of view. Could such an approach be used in news? In essence, it already is. Most news stories revolve around people's different perceptions, but how these perceptions are presented is another matter. Overtly separating stories into chunks on the basis of perspective rather than, say, subject heading is still an under-developed technique in online news writing and story construction.

The segmented approach of online should also lend itself to using different writing styles within one story. Yet how often does this happen? Newspaper journalists often cover stories which are 'hard' news but with a strong level of 'human interest'. Unless doing a special, they are usually expected to encapsulate all elements within one story and, therefore, one style. Changing writing style from straight news to narrative, for example, within a single newspaper story is not recommended practice.

Covering the same story for the Web, you will chunk and then write. You can use the hard news style for your latest factual

---

[8] Published in 1998.(www.members.aol.com/crich13/poynter1.html)

development, then narrative in a separate chunk to 'humanize' the story. This separation frees you to adopt different writing styles tailored to the content. You can even extend this flexibility to other elements of your storytelling, such as multimedia. Summaries from the reporter could be used for the audio and video on the linear kernel, with eye-witness interviews for the 'human interest' section to complement the narrative writing. As Leah Gentry says, you are able to work with the medium.

All this is fine, but how often does it happen? Carole Rich is right to call for experimentation. However, the reality is that vision is often the first casualty of the daily grind and with it falls innovation. The search is still on for a viable and reliable revenue model from online publishing, particularly online news. As was noted in Chapter 1, cutbacks started to kick in 2001, with sites folding and reductions in editorial staff. As result, the pressures mitigating against innovation increase daily.

It is as important to be pragmatic as it is easy to be idealistic about the potential and practice of online journalism, but we must also look at the bigger picture and remember what got online journalism off the ground in the first place – innovation. What was once innovatory, for example the combination of multimedia, interactivity and linkage, is now commonplace. If we want the commonplace to have developed in five years' time, we must innovate now.

In the meantime, we can consider what we do have at our disposal to assist our digital storytelling. Let us move on to explore those distinctive aspects of online that go beyond the writing – immediacy, global reach and multimedia in outline; and then the real powerhouses of archiving, interactivity and linkage in more detail.

Leverage those strengths

Transferring from one medium to another can be a salutary experience for any journalist. The established newspaper reporters who move to radio or television soon learn what they can take with them and what they have to leave behind.

The core journalistic skills of spotting, sourcing and developing a story are still essential, but the methods of constructing a story, say for television, can be very different. The factors that create this difference are rooted within the medium itself and so impinge on the whole journalistic process. For example, the television journalist will look for pictures from the outset to construct them into a sequence that will tell the story. Only then will he or she turn to words, writing a script to support and enhance the pictures.

As the medium determines the *process* of story construction, it also shapes the final *product*. Television demands the primacy of pictures and has a linear process of dissemination. Viewers of a news story are fed a single stream of content which they cannot re-order or select from (this will change with the onset of interactive television, but this linearity has dominated the process of television journalism since its inception and is still the norm today).

Put those together and you present the television journalist with an interesting challenge, namely how to get an audience and keep it. Television news asks a lot of viewers – to be passive recipients, physically committed (sitting, watching and listening) and more emotionally and intellectually engaged in a story on local government than the football, film or game show on the other channels.

Television journalists adopt a low-risk strategy to cope with this problem. Keep it short. Don't give the audience time to get bored. Tell the story, no matter how complex, in a maximum of two minutes. So, again, the medium has fundamental consequences for story construction. For example, in this case, no interview extract can be longer than ten seconds. It is also the reason why good television journalism is so difficult to do and such a comparatively rare commodity.

Do the same rules apply to online? How much does interactivity, and the power it gives to the user, affect the process of online journalism. What impact do the other distinctive elements of digital storytelling have on the end product? And how do you harness them effectively to make them work for both the content provider and user?

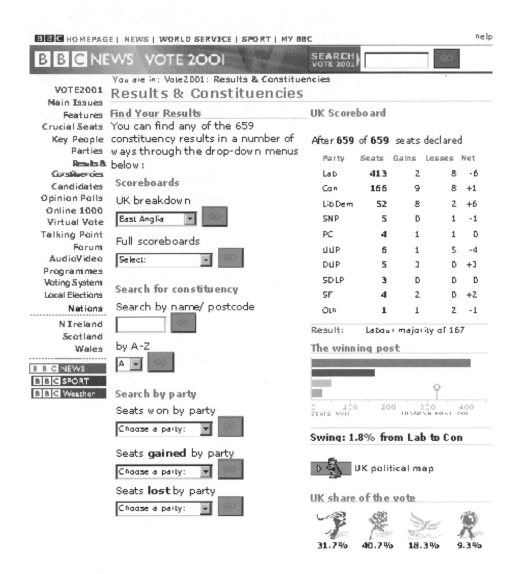

Figure 5.1: Leveraging those strengths – the BBC took full advantage of the Web's capacity as a user-driven medium with their 2001 UK General Election results service. It received more hits than any other over results night and the following day.

Immediacy

Radio and rolling television news programmes pride themselves on their immediacy. Yet they do not have the flexibility of online. As television is a linear medium, rolling news channels have to repeat a great deal of material in order to keep providing the latest summary and updates. For the person who wants an instant update, the difference between rolling news and online is like the difference between jumping on a passing bus or flagging down a taxi. The bus gets you there in the end, but you take in a lot of other scenery enroute.

However, if online news operations have the potential to be direct and immediate, they do not always exploit it. Newspapers in particular require an organizational and cultural shift to take advantage of the immediacy of online. The rhythm of a daily newspaper office, with its peaks and troughs, does not provide the continuity required for consistent online news provision. You cannot run such a service if most members of your editorial team are winding down by mid-afternoon. It requires organizational change.

Cultural barriers also limit the potential for immediacy. The tension between holding or breaking stories online before they make the paper is still apparent for many online newspapers.

Immediacy is a big factor in online journalism, but it is not as simple as turning on a tap. As Bob Eggington, the launch and project director for BBC News online, put it:

> Keeping a big, up-to-date news site going is a massive task and is harder than working in any of the established media, not least because it's always live. You print something and it stays there. But you've got to keep the site up-to-date and it's a very difficult job.[9]

Global reach

All major news organizations deal in world news. They attempt, however superficially, to have a global perspective, either in their world news section or integrated within their main news agenda

[9] Interview with author, June 2000.

and programmes. Yet no popular medium can match the Internet for global *reach*, a fact that has implications for both the news agenda and newsgathering capabilities of online news providers.

If a news site sets out to cover world events, it will soon find out via e-mails and discussion boards if it is not getting it right. Ignorance and narrow-mindedness in the newsroom are exposed to the spotlight of worldwide audiences who can tell you in an instant what they think. Mindful of their global audience, some news sites make sure world news is on the front page of their site each day. This simple act has forced many news organizations and the journalists within them to re-evaluate their news agendas.

Global reach is the most automatic of the distinctive strengths of online. It does not have to be introduced or manufactured by the journalist, as it is a fact of Internet life. However, its implications need to be understood. Global reach does not just mean the big picture. It also means millions of little pictures. Global = local.

This raises an interesting question about the Web's position as a mass medium. The Web is used by millions everyday. But it contains a multitude of different sites, each presenting a different product and experience for users. Each user can build their own relationships and networks between these sites. A bespoke rather than a mass product. And what happens when all users want the same products simultaneously (for example, visiting their favourite news site during a major breaking story)? The system can't cope and they are denied access. The Web has global reach and mass consumption, but not a mass product or the capacity for the collective reception of a single message that typifies mass media such as television.

Multimedia

The multimedia picture is patchy at present. Among the major news providers, sites such as CNN and BBC News sit on a digital goldmine of content from their broadcast operations. They offer it effectively online and generate much traffic. For them and those like them, video in particular will grow in importance as the quality and speed of delivery improves. But for others, it remains

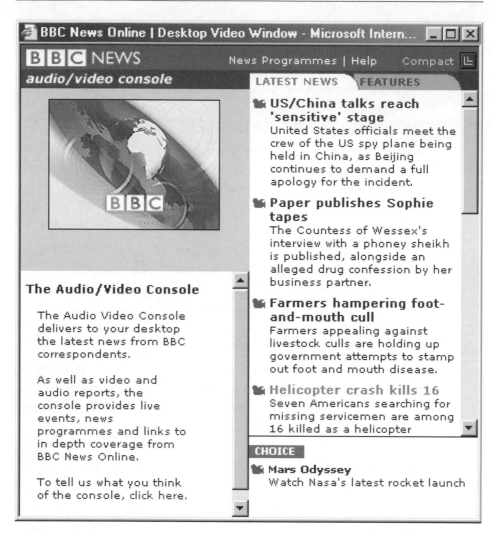

Figure 5.2: Audio and video are becoming major content features for sites that have plenty of them and can present them well, such as this BBC site.

a black hole. In theory, it is a small thing to equip your reporter with a mini disc recorder as well as a notepad. Yet, in practice, many print-based news operations have, at best, only tinkered with audio and video. As the market becomes more discerning, the established news brands may decide to become more specialized and play to their distinctive strengths. It is hard to see multimedia becoming universal at this level, apart from, of course, the use of graphics.

For the smaller operation, the take-up is even patchier, but the potential is still there. Despite the cultural and organizational barriers at the major newspapers, it is relatively easy to gather and distribute audio in particular. It is an almost completely unused facility on non-news sites, outside the entertainment sector. Why do charity sites not have appeals in audio? Why do travel sites not provide audio brochures? Why do all sites not have audio alternatives for the visually impaired?

There are distinct advantages to accessing audio and video online. These include:

- the ability to find it (you can seek out the audio and video that interests you);
- the flexibility of access (you can choose when to watch or listen)
- the range of access (you can hear and see material that you would not otherwise be able to, for example broadcasts from other countries not available on cable or satellite); and
- the storage capacity (you can listen to it again and again).

These are issues of access, but what about innovation, particularly within online journalism? There are some examples. BBC News Online reported live from the funeral of King Hussein of Jordan by combining a live video feed with Arabic commentary from the BBC World Service's Arabic Service.

Web radio has also taken off. To a degree, it has democratized the power to communicate through the audio medium. Once again, however, it has been a delivery innovation rather than an editorial one. In the main, news organizations have yet to push the boundaries of multimedia, particularly at the story level.

For example, if it became standard practice to offer the full interview as well as the soundbite, it might do wonders for politicians' interview technique. For too long they have relied on the constraints of the linear medium. Reporters ask them five different questions, but they give the same single answer because they know only ten seconds of the interview will be used. When you listen to the full interview, the evasion is obvious. Of course, the voter would rarely, if ever, hear the full interview. With online they could, if it were offered. But don't hold your breath. Compared to re-purposing existing broadcast output (complete with short reports and soundbites), such use of audio is a minority market.

Archive

At first glance, archives are not a truly distinctive element of online. They have been a feature of newspapers for centuries. Many are now stored in digital form on CD-Rom and so are also searchable.

Yet scratch the surface and you start to see significant differences between the potential of the newspaper archive and a web-based resource. First, the web-based archive can be much richer with audio, video, pictures, charts and data to complement the text. Second, the scale of web-based archived material can be impressive. By mid–2000, BBC News Online alone estimated it had up to 700,000 stories in its archive with hundreds being added daily.

However, it is the third difference, namely the amount of information being accessed, which is the real eye-opener. In the case of the BBC, it is around half the total archive each week. That is up to 350,000 stories called up and read each week – about 70,000 a day. What does this tell us? Well, among other things it demonstrates that a web-based archive is a living entity, an essential element of a site's content provision. It can complement current content and enhance interactivity and personalization of information. It also shows that a site can satisfy a broader range of user demands if it organizes its archive effectively.

Organization is the key. There is already a daily tension between what Rosenfeld and Morville[10] refer to as the 'top-down' information architecture, that is the 'basic top-level structure and navigation for organizing large bodies of content, such as entire sites', and the 'bottom-up' perspective of information architecture. This is 'how you organize content at a much finer level of granularity, not whole sites, but at the level of individual documents or going further, at the level of content "chunks"'.

What happens when 'top-down' and 'bottom-up' meet in the middle? When you define content areas for sites, you are working

[10] HTTP://web.oreilly.com/news/infoarch_0100.html

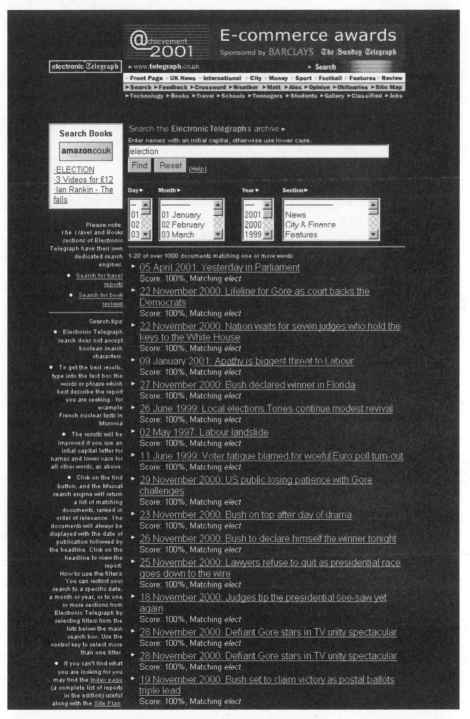

Figure 5.3: News archives are becoming increasingly valuable features of sites such as the Electronic Telegraph, which had the foresight to establish one from an early stage.

on a large canvas – broad brush rather than pointillist. How does or can this accommodate the fine detail of dividing individual stories into chunks – these 'atoms' of information.

A breaking story may be divided up into various chunks, put under a generic heading of 'Europe' or closer to home, for example, 'Wales'. This is manageable, even helpful, when you are looking at the story as a whole on the day it breaks.

The issue comes into sharper focus when you archive such a story. Do users go to a site archive for the same reason they visit the breaking news section? Or are they more interested in vertical searching, the drilling down, rather than the horizontal? If so, you have a different user group with different needs. To cater for these needs you will, of course, offer a search function. However, current site searches are not always a satisfactory way of finding material. This is because:

■ they are not always easy to find;
■ they do not always offer advanced searches;
■ if their advanced searches offer search by content category, these usually simply replicate the categories of the site (e.g. 'world' or 'uk'); and
■ some people prefer to browse directories.

Rosenfeld and Morville advocate a combination of conceptual tools (e.g. manual indexing) and technology (e.g. search engines): 'The big prize goes to those who figure out the best hybrid solution that combines the most appropriate set of technological and conceptual tools to help your particular community of users find their way to your unique content.'

One answer lies in better meta data within each story – tags in each chunk relating to archive directory headings that cut across the original top-down categories. Your user could then connect to range of information chunks within each field, not just a horizontal slice of previous pages relating to the subject-matter. You could offer that finer 'granularity' of information.

The more advanced site archives offer this flexibility, but many are overlooking one of their most precious assets and sources of unique content, namely their archives.

Linkage

The power to link lies at heart of the Web. It is the ability to read a document and then move to a completely different document, often stored on a completely different computer. This concept is based on human thought patterns. You think of one thing and that makes you think of another. However, as an individual, you are limited by the extent of your personal experience. It is difficult to think of things you do not know, unless, of course, you use that other powerful tool – your imagination. Imagination has a very firm place in the canon of journalistic skills and knowledge. However, it has its limitations if you are trying to recall factual and accurate information. In theory, with the Web, you can remove the limitations of personal experience and knowledge and plug your reader into a mainframe, built from the knowledge and experience of countless others.

In practice, of course, it can be very different. The instantaneous mental link within the brain cannot be replicated online. Download delays, broken links and irrelevant material can confound the user experience and provide headaches rather than enlightenment. So the online journalist must think carefully about which links to offer and provide them in a user-friendly or even intuitive way, whilst also making sure that the simple mechanics work.

Fundamentally, there are two type of links – internal and external.

Internal links are:
- navigational links that guide the user around the site, such as the Home button;
- links that take users to other sections of the same story or to additional features such as audio files; and
- links that take people to similar stories on the same site or the site archive.

External links are those to other sites.

All of these links are critical in facilitating that 'intuitive' process. The site that has inconsistent or confusing navigation is less likely to keep its users long enough to engage in any meaningful journey through the content. Links within a story need to be clear and reinforce the structure of the story, guiding the user through its segmentation.

However, it is perhaps the links to other stories, the archive or external sites, that need the most constant vigilance. There is a school of thought that says linking to external sites from your own is not a good idea. It is encouraging your users to leave and possibly not return. However, the Internet is not like that. If you treat your users like visitors to a car showroom, pinning them against the bonnet with the hard sell, they will go and never return. If instead you stand outside your front door, handing out details of all the best deals in town, updated every day, you will see them again and again.[11] The important lesson here is to consider what the users need and give it to them clearly and simply. In that way, external links can provide 'added value' to your site.

Bob Eggington believes that providing links for readers is one of the 'compelling differences between the Web and other media':

> You can point the reader to all the primary sources on other web sites and say 'If you don't like our take on the story, or want to check it out, or want to make your own mind up, go to the primary sources. We'll give you the pointers.'
>
> So we're not just trying to hold the audience on our own site. We're also saying there's a lot of other stuff, primary stuff, that you can go out and find for yourself, for research or verification.[12]

Ethical considerations

Another important question to ask when linking to external sites is 'What am sending my user to?' There can be a conflict of interest here for the online journalist. Any attempt to deny user access to information, including links, appears to fly in the face of the medium itself.

---

[11] You may not sell many cars, of course, and this is one of the greatest problems of the online news industry – the search for a viable business model and revenue streams.

[12] Interview with author, June 2000.

However, there are occasions when the nature of the story you are covering should at least make you reflect on any links you provide. For example, if you were writing a story about the discovery of a paedophile ring, would you link to its site as a primary source? If so, does that in some way implant some sort of relationship, however tenuous between your site and the ring's?

Libertarians will argue that it is pointless to deny your users the link because they are only two clicks away from the site anyway – one click to a search engine and the second to the site. All you will do, they believe, is drive readers away from your site and so any possible counter arguments you have presented in your responsible coverage.

Others believe that if people wish to seek out such material, it is not the business of a news organization to facilitate the process or to provide a platform for such groups. What would be the position of the news organization if it later emerged that paedophiles had used the link on your site to make contact with like-minded people and this had led to the abuse of children?

There is also the possibility that material on certain sites breaks laws regarding obscenity or the incitment of racial hatred. A link to these could be seen as aiding and abetting such violations.

Political unrest and conflict can also raise issues about linking to external sites. A country can be isolated politically and its policies receive wide criticism, but news organizations may still link to its official news sites to let readers judge for themselves. They may seek 'balance' in the links they offer just as they will in their storytelling. Thus, they will link to both sides in any conflict.

News organizations usually accept that they have responsibilities to the societies within which they operate. However, this can cause real tensions within the online medium. Any potential conflicts of interest are usually dealt with on a case-by-case basis. Online news gathering and publishing is a continuous process, with different people frequently working on the same story. Large organizations need policies on linking and other matters to ensure editorial continuity.

An example of such policies are the BBC Online Producer guidelines. These make it clear that any links to external sites should be 'editorially justifiable'. Issues uppermost in the mind of the BBC journalist should be 'editorial integrity' and 'taste and decency'. The guidelines stress the importance of checking the content of sites before linking to them. However, the challenge of controlling the web re-emerges with the edict that all linked sites should continue to be checked after the link has been established.

Despite all these safeguards, the BBC still issues its standard disclaimer on its site, distancing itself from the content of any linked site and absolving itself of any responsibility for what may be found there. The BBC is totally committed to online, but it's used to having total control over its own output. Auntie is still a little nervous about online, in case the new family pet turns out to be a rabid dog.

Interactivity

This is the final distinctive feature of online and arguably its most powerful.

People sometimes talk about interactivity with a capital 'I', as if it were some defined entity. But interactivity is a process rather than a product. Like most processes, it can operate at different levels. An understanding of those levels will help you to build interactivity into a story or site. If you apply an inappropriate level of interactivity to your story/site, you may suffer rejection; and in the case of the empty message board on a site, that can be very public.

To understand the different levels of interactivity, it is useful to think of the different models of mass communication.

The one-way model

This is the traditional model used by newspapers and broadcasters. They make decisions on what is newsworthy and what is not and then send the resulting stories to their readers who read/watch/listen or do not bother, depending on the choices the journalist has made. It is predominantly a one-way model – journalist to user. Nothing much comes back.

The two-way model

This, as it suggests, not only allows the journalist to send something, but also allows something to come back from the user. This is the beginning of interaction. However, there can be two levels of interaction within the two-way model.

- At the first level, something is coming back from the user. It is the choices the users make about what they want to see and hear based on the non-linear consumption model. They are taking control of what they consume, but they are still only consuming.
- At the second level, the user starts to contribute as well as consume. The interaction is still two way – between journalist and user – but the user becomes the provider as well as the consumer. Most journalists, including those working on hard copy newspapers, have now embraced e-mail. Some provide their e-mail address at the end of by-lined articles. This is because journalists are above all pragmatists and will embrace any new technology if they can see the benefit. It only takes a couple of journalists to mention the great lead they got on a story from a reader's e-mail to have the rest clamouring at the news editor's desk for the same opportunity. Feedback and story ideas from readers are a primary example of the second level of interaction within the two-way communication model.

Bob Eggington has frequently seen those effects at first hand and believes that such interactivity is 'changing the face of journalism':

When something happens in any part of the world we found on BBC News that you could rely on people from the area concerned to get in touch with you almost immediately. The old way of operating in journalism was that whenever anything happened, you struggled immediately to find witnesses, corroboration and contributions from people on the scene. You were hitting the phones and you were looking up telephone books for addresses and generally scrabbling around to get information that would help you understand what had happened. . . . The Internet is beginning to turn that around. When something happens, you start to get a flurry of information in, you don't have to go looking for it. The task becomes different, to filter and check it. But that is changing journalism and the sites that make the most advantage of this will be the best and most successful in the end.[13]

Such user input can extend beyond simply reacting to events. Steve Yelvington believes that journalists can use readers as a sounding board and test bed for ideas before stories are written:

There is an opportunity for the reporter to use a web log environment and say 'Here are some facts that look to me as though they mean this . . . what do you guys think?' And then you can start a conversation with people. Some may be well informed and some may be idiots, but the journalist can then participate in that conversation, and learn more, and out of that write a piece. I think that's a wonderful model.[14]

Such user input is a step apart from the one-way model. However, the journalist is still acting as the filter. The user's contribution is being channelled through him or her. This is not the case with the three-way model.

The three-way model

This is the model that makes some journalists twitchy. They can feel the onset of virtual redundancy and they fear it will be swiftly followed by the more tangible kind.

In the three-way model, users contribute to users as well as the journalist. The triangular motif can be multiplied ad infinitum, like the model of a molecular structure. However, if we see the third point of the triangle as any other user, the three-way model suffices.

---

[13] Producer Guidelines ref.
[14] Interview with author, June 2000.

Figure 5.4: The news consumer as news provider – Megastories from Out There News is constantly seeking content contributions from non-journalists, such as this farmer whom it equipped with a video camera during the 2001 foot and mouth outbreak in the UK.

The most common expression of the three-way model is the newsgroup or message board. There are also the virtual communities, such as GeoCities or Fortune City. Here users share information and hear news without the input of the journalist, and not all of the material is lightweight.

Journalists may feel 'out of the loop', but they are not. As we saw in Chapter 3, newsgroups and message boards are a useful way of understanding users' needs, interests and pre-occupations. They can provide story ideas and contacts. Journalists are still engaged in the process but they have become users as well as providers. This is an opportunity, not a threat.

So, users can be providers, but can they be journalists? Where does self-indulgent sounding-off end and a new form of journalism begin? Are there any quality benchmarks and, if so, how can they operate?

Steve Yelvington believes such a model can be self-correcting:

> Undoubtedly some bad work is going to be done by 'untrained' journalists. But bad work is done every day by trained journalists too. We rely on the marketplace to correct that. There is a marketplace for opinion and thought and that is what I see operating on the Internet.

Yelvington cites Slashdot as an example of site users self-moderating site content. Users will post corrections to previous contributions and grade each other's submissions. If you end up with a score of zero, and users have set their filter at two and above, they may never even see your contribution.

> When the environment is open like that, it does tend to even out. If you look at the medium as just an extension of the classical open marketplace of ideas, I think it makes sense. If you look at the medium as an individual product, as the print world would tend to, then I can see that this seems like a frightening loss of control. But you never really had that control to begin with. You just thought you did.

Such interaction, and the other distinctive features of online, will add yet more colours to the journalist's palette when we turn our attention to the big picture – site design. However, first, because hypertext lies at the heart of the Web and because this book is all about removing unnecessary mystique, we will look at the wonderful world of HTML.

Further reading and references

Kim, A.J. (2000). Community Building on the Web. Peachpit Press.

Krug, S. (2000). *Don't Make Me Think*. Circle.

Murray, J. (1997). *Hamlet on the Holodeck*. MIT Press.

Nielsen, J. (1999). *Designing Web Usability*. New Riders.

Rosenfeld, L. and Morville, P. (1998). *Information Architecture*. O'Neill.

- http://acij.uts.edu.au/index.html – Online Journalist, Australia. Provided by the Australian Centre for Independent Journalism. Tools for journalists include 'Signpost to Asia and the Pacific' and the 'Online Journalists' Notebook'.
- www.contentious.com – Amy Gahran's valuable e-zine for online content creator and publishers.
- www.content-exchange.com – a digital marketplace for online content creators and publishers. Includes the Content Spotlight e-mail newsletter.
- www.megastories.com – the site of 'Out There News'.
- www.ojr.org – the site of *Online Journalism Review*, a comprehensive US-based site.
- www.planetarynews.com – Steve Outing's comprehensive site, including news, information and gateways to discussion lists on online news, online writing and online newspapers.
- www.yelvington.com – Steve Yelvington's own site with useful commentary and advice.

6 Who's afraid of HTML?

HTML – random definitions

What does HTML stand for? Depends on your viewpoint, but perhaps it should be one of the following?

- **H**orrify **T**hose **M**iserable **L**osers – for the online snob who views the novice with disdain.
- **H**elp! **T**oo **M**uch **L**ogic – for the said novice who views all things IT with fear and suspicion.
- **H**unt **T**he **M**other **L**ode – for the anorak who expects too much.
- **H**ah! **T**he **M**adcap **L**aughs – for the online anarchists who think all the above have missed the point.

HTML certainly puts up the barriers and defines your position. Although most people can tell you what it stands for – **H**yper **T**ext **M**arkup **L**anguage – they have difficulty describing what it does.

There are two schools of thought about HTML, which are best summed up in the following quotes:

> Don't you worry about it at all – with web authoring software
> . . . you don't even have to think about it.[1]

---

[1] Williams and Tollett (2000).

Although visual editors have increased in sophistication over recent years, a working knowledge of HTML is still recommended as even the best editors occasionally make mistakes with code that are easier to rectify if you have some knowledge of HTML.[2]

If you like to know which end of the car to check the oil and water, it probably will not hurt to take a peek at HTML. Then, if you like what you see, you can buy other books and start stripping the engine.

There is also a psychological benefit of considering HMTL. If you never understand the principles of HTML, there is this continual fear of being *found out*. The more you talk HTML, the harder it is to confess ignorance. The thing becomes a little monster, lurking in your psyche. Why not set it free?

HTML – some urban myths

Web aficionados will shake their head in disbelief at some of the following, but these are the nightmares of the uninitiated.

'I write HTML with a web browser.'

This is wrong, you *read* (decode) HTML with a web browser.

'I need specific web authoring software to write HTML.'

This is wrong, you can write HTML on a basic word processing or text-editing package, such as Microsoft Notepad. Indeed, the more basic the better. If you write HTML on packages such as Microsoft Word, the formatting within that software can give browsers severe indigestion when they try to read the pages. If you must use Word, save the document as a text-only format (with the extension.HTM).

[2] Whittaker (2000).

'My web browser must be connected live to the Internet to read HTML.'

This is wrong, your web browser software will read your newly written pages without any connection, but it will have to go online to download new pages from the Internet.

'My web browser will only read HTML.'

This is wrong, your browser will in fact read straight text documents, should you ever want it to.

From the above, we can define the following important principles.

1 HTML can be written on a text editor.
2 It becomes HTML when you include certain codes or tags within the text, together with the message itself. The text editor will make no sense of these, presenting them literally as the series of symbols and letters that you typed in.
3 But when your text is looked at by a web browser, it reads the tags and responds accordingly, turning your text into a web page.
4 You can also use tags to give the browser messages about layout, headings, etc.
5 This message can be understood by other people's browsers (although different types of browser have different settings). So your message can be read by millions of others.
6 If you put the right tags in your message, you can link your message to someone else's message on another web page or site. Hence the hypertext link.

What does a tag look like?

Let us look at that most profound of sentences:

The quick brown fox jumps over the lazy dog.

I have just written that sentence using Microsoft Word. It looks fine on this Word document, but there is not a lot more I can do with it.

If I went into Notepad and wrote:

```
<HTML>
<HEAD>
<TITLE>The quick brown fox jumps over the lazy dog</TITLE>
</HEAD>
</HTML>
```

then saved it as dog.htm, my web browser would make lots of use of the information in <brackets>, but would not show any of it .

The text in brackets form the tags and they provide the browser with the code it needs to display the text I want to show (The quick brown, etc.) in the way I want to show it. As it is a web browser, it would show it in a way that other similar browsers would understand. Hence, the universality of the web.

You might think that this is not particularly clever. If you send a Word document to another PC loaded with the Word software (i.e. a floppy disk), you can also read the document there. However, HTML is special for a number of reasons.

First, the HTML code can also point your browser to files where you have stored still pictures, graphics, audio and video. Second, it can present all these things on the screen in an orderly and, sometimes, attractive manner. Finally, it can tell your browser to jump to other HTML files, written by yourself or anyone else and which might be stored on different computers, whatever type of browser they use – the much-vaunted hyperlink.

So HTML is worth learning and you can see it easily by going to your favourite web site and looking at the home page. Go to the tool bar at the top of the page and click on 'View'.

You will be offered various options, including 'Source'. Click on that.

What you should then see is a separate page showing all the HTML required to put that single home page together. Start scrolling. Two minutes later, stop scrolling. You will still be on that first page of HTML. There is a great deal of it. That is why people rarely write their own HTML (known, in a touching throwback to pre-industrial times, as hand coding). They prefer automated web authoring systems such as Microsoft Frontpage and Macromedia's Dreamweaver, which write the entire HTML for them.

These are known as WYSIWYG or Wizzy-wig packages – the abbreviation stands for What You See Is What You Get. These user-friendly systems allow you to type in what you hope your page will look like in the end, without distracting you with the HTML it is generating to get the page to work. The HMTL is all there, but you just do not see it, unless you ask to.

You could create that page entirely out of hand coding, with links to the relevant graphics and picture files. On the other hand, you may be too busy with other things or perhaps you are just not interested in doing this.

You probably do not want to build the site by hand. However, if you know enough HTML to spot a problem caused by the automated system and even to try to correct it, you may have reached that rare state of harmony between man and machine. You may have got the balance right.

Exercise 1 – a simple page

Open Notepad and Internet Explorer (or whatever browser you are using) and arrange the windows so you can see both without having to switch between the two.

In Notepad, type the following and save it as HTML1.htm

```
<TITLE>Small Document </TITLE>
<P> This is a test to see what the minimum HTML code will
display on a browser.
```

Open the file in your browser and view the result.

You do not need very much code to display text on the screen. The < > symbols surround the tags that tell the browser how to display a page. So 'Small Document' is put in the title bar.

The browser reads the HTML file character, line by line, in a process called 'parsing'. So the use of spaces is very limited. Put more than one space between words and the browser will ignore all but the first space. You can try this by typing in the following and saving it as HTML1b.htm

```
<TITLE> Small document </TITLE>
<P> This is a test to see what        the minimum HTML
code will display on a browser.
```

Open the file in your browser and view the result.

The text has not changed. To put in a space other than the normal gap between words, you need to indicate that you want a non-breaking space – . There are several of these special characters in HTML.

Try typing the following.

```
<TITLE> Small document </TITLE>
<P> This is a test       to see what the
minimum HTML code will display on a browser.
```

Save it as HTML2.htm and view the result.

Exercise 2 – an HTML template

In Exercise 1 we saw just how little coding was needed to get a page to display. However, there is usually a set layout for an HTML file. The following HTML is the bare minimum that should be included in any file you create.

In Notepad, type the following and save it as Template.htm

```
<HTML>
<HEAD>
<TITLE> Your title here </TITLE>
</HEAD>
<BODY>
Type your text here
</BODY>
</HTML>
```

By saving this as a template file, you can create files quickly without having to type the basic tags from scratch every time.

The <HTML> and </HTML> tags at the beginning and end denote the start and end of the HTML content of the file.

The <HEAD> tags indicate the header section of the file. They contain information that needs to be loaded first, such as the title (very important) and any META information.

The <BODY> tags denote the content part of the file. This is where most of your text and code will go. In general, anything you want to be displayed should be placed between the <BODY> tags.

Adding comments to your code

As you complete these exercises, you will create files to refer to later as a guide to the various tags to use. Adding comments is essential to help you understand what you have written. This is done by using the following:

```
<!–add any comment you like here–>
```

Exercise 3 – changing the look of text

You can create web pages by using the simple template from Exercise 2 above, but they will not be very interesting to look at. However, you can change the appearance of the text on screen by using some simple tags to give some variety.

In Notepad, load Template.htm and type the following.

```
<HTML>
<HEAD>
<TITLE>Different styles of text</TITLE>
</HEAD>
<BODY>
<b>This is bold</b>
but this
<em>is emphasized</em> which is the same as
<i>italics.</i>
<strong>This may look like bold but its a different tag.</strong>
```

And <u>this</u> and <s>this</s> are obvious.
</BODY>
</HTML>

Save it as HTML3.htm and view the result.

Looking at the page, you can see how the <b> and the <strong> tags and the <em> and <i> are similar. Both work well with Internet Explorer and Netscape, so you can choose which to use. The <u> tag is a straight underline function. Do not forget that hyperlinks are shown underlined. So it may be confusing to a user to see an underlined piece of text.

The <s> tag denotes a strike through, which is common in legal documents where any alterations or changes need to be shown. It is also a useful reminder of why HTML was developed in the first place – not as a design tool but as a method of putting documents on the Internet.

Exercise 4 – paragraphs, breaks and formatting

Although HTML is not a layout language, we do need a method for dividing the blocks of text that appear.

In Notepad, load Template.htm and type the following.

```
<HTML>
<HEAD>
<TITLE>Paragraphs and breaks</TITLE>
</HEAD>
<BODY>
type lots of text here<p>
and lots more text here<p>
type lots of text here<br>
and lots more text here<br>
</BODY>
</HTML>
```

Save it as HTML4.htm and view the result.

You can see the difference between the <p> and the <br> tags, but note that there are no closing tags on these. You can add them if you wish, but they are not necessary.

Load Template.htm again and type the following.

```
<HTML>
<HEAD>
<TITLE>Pre-formatting</TITLE>
</HEAD>
<BODY>
<PRE>
LA LA LA LA
I AM SO HAPPY
LA LA LAAA LA
     VERY HAPPY SONG
     by Andy
</PRE>
</BODY>
</HTML>
```

Save it as HTML4a.htm and view the result.

This kind of formatting is popular for use with song lyrics and poetry on the web. But text placed in a <PRE> tag is displayed in a fixed font and without images. You can place 'style' tags like <b> and <i> within the tags, but it is still quite limited.

Exercise 5 – headings

Headings are another important feature of presenting text and you can also do these with HTML.

In Notepad, load Template.htm and type the following.

```
<HTML>
<HEAD>
<TITLE>Headings</TITLE>
</HEAD>
<BODY>
<H1>Heading1</H1>
```

```
<H2>Heading2</H2>
<H3>Heading3</H3>
<H4>Heading4</H4>
<H5>Heading5</H5>
<H6>Heading6</H6>
</BODY>
</HTML>
```

Save it as HTML5.htm and view the result.

Load Template.htm again and type the following.

```
<HTML>
<HEAD>
<TITLE>Headings2</TITLE>
</HEAD>
<BODY>
<big>O</big>nce upon a time there was a <small>little</small> mouse. </BODY>
</HTML>
```

Save it as HTML5a.htm and view the result.

Unlike the <H> tag which needs no <p> or <br> tag, the <big> and <small> tags can be included directly in the text.

Change the HTML in HTML5b.htm to include the following.

```
<big>O</big>nce upon a <H1>time<H1> there was a <small>little</small> mouse.
```

Save it as HTML5b.htm and view the result. Notice how the <H> tag forces a new line, upsetting the formatting.

The <H> tag is an easy way of changing the size of text. You will also notice that the text is bold. This tag works quite well as a quick way of defining a section of text or chapter heading. Note, however, that the <big> and <small> tags are relative sizes depending upon the base font size or the font size to which your browser defaults. So this is not the most effective way to control fonts. For that we need another tag.

Exercise 6 – font size, colour and typefaces

The <font> tag allows you to change the typeface, size and colour of your text, just like the font utility in a word processor. To address those, the tag has several additional elements or attributes.

In Notepad, load Template.htm and type the following.

```
<HTML>
<HEAD>
<TITLE>The font tag</TITLE>
</HEAD>
<BODY>
<font size=+3>big stuff</font>
<font color=red>in bright colours</font>
can often scare. But both <font color=blue size=+5>can be
very effective</font>
</BODY>
</HTML>
```

(UK readers should note the spelling of 'color' in the HTML.)

Save it as HTML6.htm and view the result.

Add the following line to the code you just typed.

```
<font face="arial"> big stuff</font>
```

Save it as HTML6a.htm and view the result.

The text should appear in the Arial typeface. Arial is a very common font, present on most PCs. If you were to use an obscure font for your page, it would not display on machines that do not have that font. All the <font> tag does is tell the receiving computer which typeface to use. If it has not got it, it cannot show it.

One solution is to use very common fonts, but you can also use the generic names for fonts.

Load up TEMPLATE.htm and type the following.

```
<HTML>
<HEAD>
<TITLE>The font tag cont.</TITLE>
</HEAD>
```

```
<BODY>
<P><Font face="sans-serif">sans-serif</font>
<P><Font face="serif">serif</font>
<P><Font face="cursive">cursive</font>
<P><Font face="fantasy">fantasy</font>
<P><Font face="monospace">monospace</font>
</BODY>
</HTML>
```

Save it as HTML6b.htm and view the result.

You may find that some of the selections do not seem to change, but try it on several computers and compare the results. All the machines should display the serif, sans serif and monospace fonts, but the cursive and fantasy may not display. This is further proof that HTML is not meant to be a 'design' tool.

Exercise 7 – alignment

Having decided on the font, its size and colour, how will it be presented on the screen? HTML does have some alignment features, but they are very limited.

Load up TEMPLATE.htm and type the following.

```
<HTML>
<HEAD>
<TITLE>Alignment</TITLE>
</HEAD>
<BODY>
<center>Centred text is formal<p>
but dull</center>
<p align=left>Left seems natural, because we read from left
to right<br>
and it has a strong line on the left to orientate us.<p>
<p align=right>Right alignment can be hard to read because
the left-hand side often <br>
has a jagged feel, losing that straight edge that orientates us
as we read.
</BODY>
</HTML>
```

Save it as HTML7.htm and view the result.

(UK readers should note the spelling of 'center' in the HTML.)

Try re-sizing the browser window. The relative position stays the same and the alignment does not change, but the effect of the alignment, especially on the right, is lost as the window gets smaller.

Exercise 8 – colour on the page

Using colour is a good way to communicate a message. For many, black is serious, blue is cold, and red and oranges are warm colours. You can use HTML to add different colours to your page.

Load up HTML6.htm and amend the <Body> tag so it looks like the following.

```
<BODY BGCOLOR=RED>
```

Save it as HTML8.htm and view the result.

You can see that a bright red background has appeared. Red is one of a small set of colours which can be described in HTML by their names, rather than a code. The others are black, gray, silver, white, maroon, yellow, olive, pink, green, lime, aqua, teal, navy, blue, purple, fuchsia and orange. All other shades of colour are described by a series of numbers and letters decided by something called the hexadecimal method.

If you change the background colour, you must make sure it does not make the text impossible to read. The colour of the font is as important as the background colour and is a key consideration in your design. In general, a lighter background colour with a darker font colour works best.

Exercise 9 – the missing link

There's been much talk in this book on the ability of HTML to link you from one document to another. But how do you write that instruction into a page?

In Notepad, type the following:

```
<HTML>
<HEAD>
<TITLE>Links</TITLE>
</HEAD>
<BODY>
<A HREF="http://www.uclan.ac.uk">The University of Central Lancashire web site</A>
</BODY>
</HTML>
```

When you view the page, the words 'The University of Central Lancashire web site' will appear in blue and underlined, representing a live hypertext link. The URL 'www.uclan.ac.uk' does not appear. That is just the destination for the link.

Exercises – in conclusion

There are many other HTML tags, for example those that show images on the page, but these are enough to get you started. It may also be enough to make you decide that you will never learn a lot of HTML, preferring the authoring packages such as Dreamweaver and Front Page. It may be that you have looked at this and found HTML boring. However, if boredom has replaced fear, this chapter will have served a purpose.

Further reading and references

Castro, E. (2000). *HTML 4*. Peach Pit Press.

Raggett, D. (ed.) (1998). *Raggett on HTML 4*. 2nd edition. Addison-Wesley.

Whittaker, J. (2000). *Web Production*. Routledge.

Williams, R. and Tollett, J. (2000). *The Non-Designers Design Book*. 2nd edition. Peach Pit Press.

7 Design your web resource

'Computer – take away two wrong answers and leave us with the right answer and the one remaining wrong answer please.'

Chris Tarrant, presenter of the TV quiz programme 'Who wants to be a millionaire'

Bookshelves groan with the weight of opinion on web design. If you are looking for guidance, it can be a confusing and intimidating process. You may have climbed the mountain of information retrieval in Chapter 3. But now you are in a jungle, full of warring tribes. And you don't even speak the language.

Before we proceed, we had better get to know the natives.

Conflicting views and common ground

People are excited about web design. Consequently, they care and have strong, but sometimes conflicting, opinions. This is fine but can be confusing for the new arrival. This divergence of view is often characterized as 'art versus engineering' or the 'stucturalists versus the designers'. Note the 'versus'.

Take, for example, Jakob Nielsen. He is currently the best-known usability guru within the web world. An 'evangelist at heart', he believes the primary function of a web resource is to meet the needs of the user as simply and speedily as possible. Content –

usually concise text – is king. Navigation is 'a necessary evil' and graphics should be kept to a minimum. A favourite Nielsen aphorism is 'Remove graphic; increase traffic. It's that simple.' He has even argued for the 'end of web design', claiming that sites must 'tone down their individual appearance and distinct design'. Can't be much clearer than that. So he gets put in the blue corner.

In the red corner, you might find someone like David Siegel.[1] Just the title of his best-known book, *Creating Killer Web Sites* (1997), gives you an inkling that he doesn't live on the same block as Jakob Nielsen.

Then you read the preface, which promises 'a thrilling jeep-drive through the Style Sheet landscape, with pitfalls, pinnacles and perilous browser implications around every corner', and you question whether in fact he lives on the same planet as Nielsen.

Are these two people really talking about the same thing? Well, in essence, they are, but from very different perspectives. However, there is also some common ground.

You might guess that the following quote comes from Siegel: 'the scientific method can only take you so far. There is still a need for inspiration and creativity in design.' In fact, it comes from Nielsen.

Again, you might guess who said: 'It is the designer's responsibility to present content appropriately' It was actually David Siegel, between jeep rides.

I'm being selective with my quotes, not to propose a revisionist perspective on Nielsen and Siegel but instead to make a much simpler point. It's not helpful to sanctify or demonize either of them. It's too easy to portray the usability experts as

---

[1] There have been reports that Siegel has had a 'change of heart' over his design beliefs. Lighthouse on the web (www.shorewalker.com/pages/siegel_turns–1.htm) even went so far as to announce that he had 'joined the Nielsen camp', disillusioned by problems with browser technology. If so, he has not taken any of his original sites down, and his book *Creating Killer Web Sites* still sells in large numbers and continues to provoke debate. Reviews among Amazon readers in mid-2000 either hailed Siegel's book as 'historically important' and 'still cutting edge after all these years' or 'disappointing' and 'outdated'. The point is that Siegel's original concepts, whether he wishes them to be or not, are still influential and represent a 'Siegel' school of thinking as expounded in this chapter.

the buttoned-down control freaks and the designers as the free spirits. In fact, it is David Siegel who talks of reaching out to users, enticing them, leading them into sites. It is Jakob Nielsen who says the user must roam where he or she wishes and if the user is controlled, it will feel 'harsh and dominating'.

So everything is not always as it seems. Jakob Nielsen would no more countenance a 'perilous browser implication' than fly to the Moon. Yet they do share a common view on design. They both see it as the way to *communicate*. It is just that they believe in communicating in different ways and sometimes even different things.

So remember that both views have value. Avoid stereotypes and do not close your mind. It is poor journalistic practice, particularly when working within the online medium, because:

- The Web is an immature medium. Dogma is always unhealthy, but here it is particularly suspect. Designers offer 'solutions', but it is easier to be certain about bad practice than good. You can measure the bad (i.e. user disenchantment), whereas satisfaction is not so quantifiable.
- The Internet can deliver an enormous diversity of web content to an unparalleled range of audience. Is there one design solution for this rich mix? Is it not a contradiction of the medium to demand just one way to design web resources?
- Web design engages with a wide range of disciplines, skills and processes. A flexible outlook about the end product from such a process is surely helpful.

So let's skirt around the natives and plot our own course through the jungle. Let's focus on design as a means of communication. Why? Because it is. But also because, as such, it is a continuation of the journalistic process we are examining in this book.

Just as we identify and gather news and other content and then select it, we must also present it online. We have looked at how to maximize the power of the medium when we construct a single story, now we must continue that process through to delivery. In other words, we must consider how to communicate our story through the online design.

To do this, we must step back and look at the site as a whole. web design cannot be decided on a chunk-by-chunk or story-by-story basis. You will face interesting questions about how the construction of each single story relates to the organization of the whole site, but first you must have an organizational structure for your site. This and other fundamentals should lead your content presentation, not be led by it. So we have to look at design at the site level.

Unfortunately, this perspective often removes the process from the orbit of the journalist or content provider, despite the fact that design is an integral part of communicating your message. As online content specialist Amy Gahran remarks:

> Web content still gets treated as an afterthought much of the time. Sometimes, development teams perceive content as a kind of lump that magically appears and then must be packaged in the best possible way, regardless of its condition or value. Other times development teams view content as filler that will be poured in *after* they have created the perfect site design.[2]

So if it does not seem 'real world' to devote part of a book on journalism online to site design and development, let me suggest that:

- this view will have to change because of the importance of content;
- change will be assisted by journalists and content providers understanding the process of site development and making positive contributions/asking awkward questions, and so engaging in/forcing their way into the process; and
- content providers for small-scale web resources are already site developers without necessarily knowing the underlying principles of site design.

This is not to suggest that what follows will turn you into an information architect or graphic designer, but it will make you

---

[2] www.contentious.com

aware of the importance of these and other skills in web design. It will inform the skills audit you should undertake when developing your web resource. What can you do and what do you need help with? (Decide on this at the outset as it will avoid bottlenecks and delays later when you reach the limit of your abilities.) It will also point you in the right direction to find out more. And hopefully, it will demonstrate how your journalistic perspective can inform the whole process.

Language problems

Talk of information architects brings us to our next obstacle – a language barrier. The locals in our jungle may not get on, but they are familiar with the terrain. They would make invaluable guides, if you could just understand what they are taking about.

My flippant jungle image runs the risks of trivializing the work and thoughts of established web designers. It is not meant to. There are excellent books and web resources on this subject, some of which will be used for the framework of this chapter. Some are even paragons of clarity, but, again, there is the issue of the top-down verses bottom-up (as explored in Chapter 3). If you are offered terms such as 'information architecture', 'navigation' and 'user interface' at the bottom of your learning curve, it can feel like a steep climb. The problem is exacerbated by a tendency for these terms to be used in an interchangeable way because many of the activities they describe do overlap.

As Robin Williams and John Tollett (2000) note:

> The interface and the navigation are generally inseparable elements: if people say 'The interface is great', it probably means your site is easy to navigate; if people say 'It's so easy to navigate', they probably feel comfortable with the interface.

This is fine if you are an accomplished designer, and, as Williams and Tollett point out, it does not really matter if you are a user. The user just wants the site to work for him or her. However, if you are trying to get your head around the intricacies of web design and development for the first time, it can be a problem.

So let's look at it once again from the bottom up, rather than from the top down. What are the key stages in developing a web resource? I have identified ten.

1 Ask yourself if online is the right medium for your message.
2 Define who you are trying to communicate with and what you are trying to communicate.
3 Define your mission and the goals for your site.
4 Consider all your potential content.
5 Organize the content into sections.
6 Choose a structure for your sections.
7 Give users the tools to find their way around the sections.
8 Present the whole package effectively.
9 Ensure that the whole package works within the online environment.
10 See what your users think before going live.

These stages will guide you through the rest of this book, as you take your content through the design process.

However, this book is also intended as a primer and one of its functions is to point you to other texts, some of which are quoted later in this chapter. In these texts you will keep bumping into information architects and graphic designers. So let's consider some definitions before we move on.

Information architecture

Information architecture, as its name implies, is fundamental to your design. John Shiple[3] is in no doubt about its importance:

Information architecture (also know as IA) is the foundation for great web design. It is the blueprint of the site upon which all other aspects are built – form, function, metaphor,

---

[3] www.wired.com

navigation and interface, interaction and visual design. Initating the IA process is the first thing you should do when designing a site.

The text on this subject is called, not surpisingly, *Information Architecture* and is by Louis Rosenfeld and Peter Morville (1998). They give the information architect a wide-ranging brief, including:

1 defining the mission and vision for a site;
2 determining the content and functionality of the site;
3 specifying how users find information on the site; and
4 mapping out how the site will accommodate growth and change.[4]

When describing information architecture, designers often focus on the third role, which is specifying how users find information on the site. Rosenfeld and Morville have broken this role into the following tasks:

- designing ways to group your content;
- designing a labelling system for those content groups;
- designing navigation systems to help you move around and browse through the content; and
- designing searching systems for your content.

Navigation

Rosenfeld and Morville's definition clearly places navigation as a sub-set of information architecture. It also emphasizes the interlocking relationship between navigation, content grouping and site structure within the overall information architecture.

Navigation is the means you offer your users to locate their position within your site and find their way around the structure, both forwards and back again. It gives them something to hold on to and, if you get it right, it will increase both their confidence in your site and their ability to use it.

[4] Rosenfeld and Morville (1998), p. 11.

Jakob Nielsen (1999) poses the following three fundamental questions of navigation on a web site.

- Where am I?
- Where have I been?
- Where can I go?

He also points out that it is not just a matter of putting up the right signposts:

> No matter what navigation design you pick for your site, there is one common theme to all navigation. All it does is visualize the user's current location and alternative movements relative to the structure of the underlying information space. If the structure is a mess, then no navigation design can rescue it.

Users like to build a mental picture of the organization of a site. This is not possible if there is no proper structure. As Lynch and Horton (1999) remark:

> Web sites are built around basic structural themes. These fundamental architectures govern the navigational interface of the web site and mould the user's mental models of how the information is organized.

User interface

Jennifer Fleming (1998) states that:

> For successful navigation design, it's important to consider the interface as well ... In the graphical environment of the web, interface design has to do with constructing visual meaning. The happy marriage of architecture and interface – of logical structure and visual meaning – creates a cohesive user experience. The marriage is crucial to helping users get around on the web.

The user interface can extend, for example, to how well or badly you have labelled your content sections. If the labelling is ambiguous, you are making it more difficult for the user to operate within the environment of your site. However, with the web, as Fleming points out, the focus is on making sense of the environment generated by the medium, with its interactive and graphic capacity.

You can structure your content logically and provide the right navigational aids, but how your user is able to relate to them and work them is the key ingredient of interface.

User interface can be everything from having standard colours for visited links to using metaphors that help deliver the other elements of the information architecture (e.g. content categories and navigation). You may use the disciplines of graphic design to present your interface, but they are not your interface design. That should centre on functionality and utility.

Graphic design

To some beginners, this *is* web design, i.e. the layout, use of typeface, colour and graphics. It is in fact just one stage of the process, but a critical one.

Being a graphic designer must be a frustrating business. To the uninitiated it looks easy because the tools of the graphic designer are at the top of the box. You can change the font and text layout with the click of a mouse, even on a basic word processing package. This gives people the false impression that as they can 'do a little graphic design', they can try it on a web page. This is not the case.

There is a good argument for saying that if you only have enough budget to call in a single expert for your web project, you should make it a graphic designer. It is a highly skilled discipline, particularly on the web, which is not a sympathetic environment for graphic designers. It is difficult for them to control how the same page is seen by every user because, among other things, not every user uses the same type of web browser. Graphic designers *hate* not being in control so they have spent a lot of time learning how to control the digital beast. Becoming a homemade graphic designer on a web site can be like being a lion tamer for a day, with the same messy consequences.

Usability experts

Usability is now a big issue in the web world. The current thinking goes something like: 'The novelty has worn off. It's no big deal to go online any more. Expectations have risen and choice has been extended. Sites must deliver.'

A good way to test whether a site is delivering the goods is constantly to check with your users and consult a usability expert if you wish. But don't restrict usability to information-based content. If an entertainment site is not entertaining, it's got a usability problem.

So, returning to the ten key stages, depending on who you read, 2–7 fall within the field of information architecture, 7 is also navigation, 8 is graphic design and layout, 9 is user interface and 10 is user testing.

And 1 is just a question – but it is well worth asking.

Is online the right medium for my message?

'Scuse me, while I kiss the sky . . .' Jimi Hendrix, 'Purple Haze'

Everything starts with an idea and lots of big 'blue sky' questions. But the most important question is often forgotten – 'is online the right medium for my message'?

Everyone who has written a book about the Internet has felt compelled to address what Nicholas Negroponte (1996) called 'the paradox of a book'. The question being 'Why commit your thoughts on the power of the Internet to thin wafers of dead tree?'

The arguments are well rehearsed. Books, magazines and newspapers are more portable, more tactile and more intimate, and they are usually easier to read. By contrast, the computer interface is 'primitive – clumsy at best and hardly something with which you might wish to curl up in bed' (Negroponte, 1996).

As Jakob Nielsen (1999) points out, 'the web is not good for very long documents that need to present a steadily progressing argument'. Books are better for this.

For some people, the new media versus old media debate has degenerated into trench warfare, particularly in the field of newspaper journalism. 'Dead Tree Dailies' or traditional newspapers have either absolutely no future or a noble, glorious one, depending on whom you listen to. Online versus traditional. Note the 'versus' again.

This debate is not helpful because, once again, it polarizes positions and closes minds. Thankfully, it is not within the scope of this book, but it can serve one useful purpose. It should remind you there are alternatives to the online medium and you should consider using these as well as, or even instead of, going online.

The important thing is to ask that first question. Pause for thought.

So how do you decide? Well, by asking more questions; in fact, the same questions that will shape your online content, should you choose to go down that road. In particular,

- who am I trying to communicate with?
- what message am I trying to communicate?

These questions sound simplistic, but the answers can be complex. For example, considerations of 'who' should include not only the specific interests and information needs of your users, but also their technical capacity to receive your message.

So let us consider what you are communicating and with whom. We must 'define it, then design it'.

Who am I trying to communicate with?

Radio journalists are often told to 'think of an individual, someone you know' when presenting the news or a programme. It is meant to personalize or naturalize the delivery. With the web, it is a bit more complicated.

For a start, the users come to you, accessing many different parts of your output in many different ways. This can make it

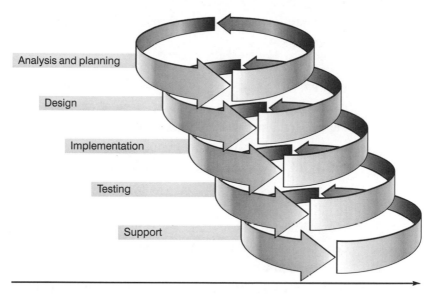

Analysis and planning

Design

Implementation

Testing

Support

Figure 7.1: The various stages in building your site occur concurrently rather than consecutively and will often also feel and look like this.

difficult to define your readership. However, sites that try to, even if they target several different user groups, are usually more successful than those that do not. Some of the user differences are specific (definably different user groups with different content demands). Some of them are generic (some users will have low-grade browsers, but you do not know who or how many). Of course, these differences overlap and will change.

So you must cater for the generic, but also focus on the specific. What you cannot do is hit and hope.

You can break your potential user differences down into three areas:

- your users' knowledge of the web;
- any technological variations of user access; and
- your users' information requirements and interests.

Users' knowledge of the web

Web users come in all shapes and sizes, with many different levels of knowledge and sophistication. Accepting the limitations of categorization, we can put web users broadly into the following three groups.

- Captive (wide-eyed innocent) – they will use your resource regardless of its presentation, design or their skill level. A captive audience will be uncritical of the work and often judge content on their preconceptions about the subject or author, rather than any intrinsic value within the content and design. Fans who visit pop star sites often fall within the captive user group.
- Non-captive (the browser) – this is probably the most common type using the web. As browsers, they look for specific information with little idea of where they can get it. Once they find it with a search engine or link, they may read the document if it gives them what they want, as long the presentation is reasonably user friendly.
- Experts (the surfer) – these look for specific information presented in a specific way. They expect sites to 'work' in a certain way and often disregard content and reject sites if they do not meet their criteria. Once they have found a site that meets their needs, they are less likely to return to it regularly like the enamoured browser. They will just add it to their bulging collection of bookmarked sites, to be monitored occasionally.

However, it should be noted that web users are chameleons. Many will fit into more than one of the above categories, depending on the subject-matter they are seeking. The expert can become a captive when trawling the fanzines of his favourite football team.

Technological variations

Designers of web pages usually have good equipment. They work on it all day and it pays the bills, so why not? They also often have the latest kit – for the same reasons, but also because some of them are in love with technology.

All of this makes them untypical users. Most users have the best equipment they can afford or the first machine they bought. PCs are reasonably durable. They do not burn out like light bulbs. They are not easy to sell second-hand, because the price and specification of the new models keeps improving. Once people make the big decision to buy a PC, many stick with what they've got for a long time. There are too many other technology products, such as mobile phones, PDAs, MP3 players, etc., pulling the pounds or dollars out of their pockets. Many also feel sufficiently technologically challenged not to consider free software upgrades.

So designers should not design for themselves, but for the users and their variable levels of technology. It is important to remember that not all web users have the capacity to receive web materials in the same way or at the same speed. If you ignore this, you will minimize, not maximize, your potential audience.

The following are some potential technological variations to consider.

- Screen size – a designer may work off a 21-inch monitor, but most users will have 17-inch screen unless of course they are reading off their mobile phone.
- Type and age of the browser – browsers are the software systems in your PC that interpret HTML codes and turn them into the web pages you see everyday. There are two main makes of browser – Netscape and Internet Explorer – and they interpret HTML differently. There are also different versions of each make, with different facilities and functions. You should always user test your pages to make sure they are compatible with different browsers.
- Delivery infrastructure – some users have slower modems than others. Some are connected to sluggish servers. Some even suffer from telephone systems that are not state-of-the-art. This problem was highlighted in Australia where sheep farmers live in remote rural areas. They wanted to use the web for wool market reports and other information. However, in some cases, single pages were taking up to three minutes to download, costing too much time and money. The farmers needed text,

not graphics. The Australian Broadcasting Corporation reported that one researcher surveyed 500 agricultural web sites and
only rated two with top marks for 'net appeal'.[5]

Users' information requirements and interests

This final category links most closely with the question 'What is
the message I am trying to communicate?'. It requires a definition
of what your prime users wish to get from your site. It refers to
their interests, desires and needs.

- Interests – this is particularly important to news sites. Defining
  the pre-occupations and consuming passions of your readers.
- Desires – maybe they want to be entertained rather than/as
  well as informed?
- Needs – this is particularly important for information-based
  sites. Many sites of commercial organizations simply reflect the
  corporate structure of company. They may regard their
  customers as a prime user group, but the site does not meet the
  customers' needs. This lesson is being learned the hard way on
  e-commerce sites where brochureware and hard sell is giving
  way to information and service with opportunities to buy.
  However many corporate and not-for-profit information-based
  sites still have a long way to go. The starting point is to know
  your user and put yourself in their shoes. Needs must also be
  considered from the utility perspective. We have already seen
  the advantages of breaking stories into 'chunks', but what if the
  user wants to print off the entire story as a single document?
  They should be offered this as an alternative, with the whole
  story reconstructed into a single file for easier printing.

What is the message I am trying to communicate?

In an ideal world, this question would be answered by giving your
users what interests them, what they desire and what meets their
needs. However, there are several considerations shaping this

[5] www.abc.net.au/pm/s104157.htm

calculation; most notably, your capacity to deliver what is needed and desired.

There may be logistical constraints on delivery. There is little point in designing a site that your organization cannot service. This is major issue for web content providers, particularly within the commercial sector. If your site has a 'last updated on . . .' notice which is a source of major embarrassment, take the site down. It is doing more harm than good. Instead, spend the money on a billboard on the local highway that says 'Look at us. We're useless.' At least it will provide a little shade for the local hitchhikers.

If you have problems updating your site, the fault lies in:

- not enough consideration given to content maintenance at site design stage; and/or
- inadequate commitment to content provision within the organization.

The obvious nature of these conclusions show that these are self-inflicted wounds that could have been avoided if hard-headed questions had been asked at the design stage. You must be realistic. Effective web sites that attract large readerships on a regular basis take a lot of content maintenance. They don't come about by magic.

The second constraint on delivery may be conceptual. Even sites that make the commitment still sometimes come unstuck because they are uncertain of exactly what they are trying to communicate. They may lose sight of their prime users or try to satisfy two groups of users with very different, and sometimes conflicting, interests.

We have seen that it is possible to satisfy two groups of users, but it can be problematical. It is less of an issue if you have two groups with different information demands, but what if two user groups have fundamentally different expectations of their web experience on your site? If one group wants fun and enter-tainment, how will this sit with those seeking information? Sites for car manufacturers are a good example of this dichotomy. They feel the need to be fun, strong on image and 'modern'. Yet many visitors want information on fuel consumption and insurance group. The result can be the marriage from hell.

Sometimes organizations have to recognize limitations – not of the medium, but of resolving two very different user groups. In fact, the medium can be the solution, not the problem. The answer may come from a separate, yet linked, web resource or different guided entry points on to the same site for different user groups.

Define the mission and goals for your site

Mission statements

Mission statements smack of 1980s management theory, along with 'empowerment' and 'total quality'. The concept of mission statements seems peculiarly out of time and place in today's online environment. If you are a young reader, you may not have even heard of them. However, mission statements can have their uses.

Having asked the 'who' and 'what' questions, it is now time to consider the purpose of your site and any objectives you have for it. A mission statement is a good way of summarizing your position in a form that is accessible to all the members of your team.

As Lynch and Horton (1999) observe:

The first step in designing any web site is to define your goals. Without a clear stated mission and objectives, the project will drift, bog down, or continue past an appropriate endpoint. Careful planning and a clear purpose are the keys to success in building web sites, particularly when you are working as part of a development team. This is a timely reminder that mission and objectives can guide the process as well as shape the product, acting as a valuable point of focus and reference.

If you draw up a mission statement for your site, you can compare it with the mission of your organization. Does the former serve the latter? If not, perhaps it is time for the first of your many re-thinks.

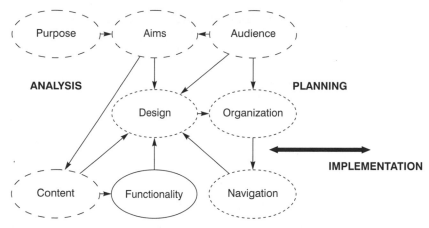

Figure 7.2: The plan for your site design must be built on an analysis of key elements such as the site's purpose and audience.

Missions tend to be broad statements, maybe only two or three sentences. Is this appropriate for your web project? Well, yes and no. If you set too many specific goals at the outset, they can later become hurdles that are difficult to negotiate. A mission statement provides a flexible enough starting point and reference point. From here on in, you have to monitor just where the process takes you. You will have to constantly refine and re-assess your ideas in the light of your original mission, which in turn may require fine tuning to ensure the relevance and viability of the final product.

So constant evaluation and some flexibility are important. However, you also need precision to manage the project, with provision for how long it will take and how any success will be measured. Thus, additional documentation will be required along the way. As Lynch and Horton (1999) remark:

> Building a web site is an ongoing process, not a one-time project with static content. Long-term editorial management and technical maintenance must be covered in your budget and production plans for the site.

Such documentation enters the realms of project management, which is also beyond the scope of this book. However, it is worth noting the importance of work plans, timetables and budgets to deliver your mission and achieve your goals.

The standard demarcation of any development process is:

- analysis and planning;
- design;
- implementation;
- testing; and
- support.

Although this is fine in principle, there is a problem when applying it as a model for web development. It gives an impression of a linear, sequential process. In reality, these stages will overlap considerably. For example, we are now reaching the end of the analysis and planning process. The model says it is time to design, but I say let's do a little testing first.

Test the dream

You have thought hard about your users and your message. And you have got yourself a mission statement. Up to this stage it has been a bit like doing a crossword puzzle; filling in the answers you know, hoping it will confirm your hunch on others you were not sure of and even provide a shaft of insight into one that is particularly troubling you.

But when do you bring all this blue sky stuff down to earth? Well after you have created your mission statement is as good a time as any. And how? Well try putting your model to the test.

You should have based as much of your early thinking as possible on solid evidence rather than speculation, but it is still necessary to test it out in two different areas.

- Against any competition – are there other sites providing a similar service? What are they doing and how? Are there any outward signs of success? What sort of users do they attract?
- Amongst your target users – you can put yourself in the shoes of your target users until you have virtual blisters, but you will still be surprised by the reactions of some real people. You should have already spoken to members of your target

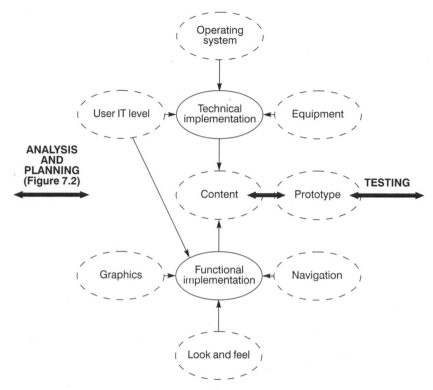

Figure 7.3: From analysis and planning to implementation.

audience at the conceptualizing stage. Now you have something to show them – your initial ideas and mission. See what they think. Do not be panicked by negative comment, but do not ignore it either. If you have to return to the drawing board, your previous work will not have been wasted. You will get back to this point much quicker next time.

But if you get green lights, move on to the next stage. Start to 'ground the blue sky', applying structure to your ideas.

Where's the PC?

This is more like it. Design. The big D. The moment we have all been waiting for. Losing our virtual virginity. Making a web site. There is a web 'designer' in all of us. Hit the keyboard. Experiment with coloured text, obscure fonts and textured backgrounds. This is design, isn't it? Well, no, actually. So log out,

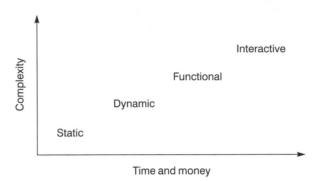

Figure 7.4: The inevitable, yet changing, relationship between content, complexity and cost.

close down, pull the plug, find a large box with a lock . . . and put your PC in it.

There is nothing to stop you playing with ideas on screen or building prototypes, but your design process should not be *driven* by this. In any case, as mentioned in the preface, there are many manuals to guide you through the mechanics of applying web authoring software. This is not one of them.

Instead, we must concentrate on the large number of fundamental questions and issues you need to consider before you set one finger on the keyboard. Only when you have thought about these carefully will you be in a position to communicate your ideas/message/news clearly. So give your computer a holiday. Instead, get a large supply of paper and pencils, an eraser and, if you want to be really hi-tech, some sticky-back reminder notes.

If you doubt the wisdom of this, spend half an hour surfing the web, looking at the web sites of small to medium-sized companies. You will find scores, hundreds, thousands of sites that do not work. They lie there, rusting hulks – moribund, neglected, unloved and unvisited.

These sites may have been 'designed' in-house by the IT team or even by outside consultants because the companies felt they needed an online presence. Too often, however, the emphasis is on bells and whistles (they impress the Chief Executive) rather than users and content. These companies made a fatal mistake. They never invested in that large box with a lock for the critical early developmental stage.

As Matt Haig, a leading e-PR practitioner in the UK, puts it in *E-PR* (2000), many businesses do not understand the 'terms' of the Internet:

> This is why so many businesses that sped headlong onto the information superhighway are now left stranded in the lay-by, alone and unvisited in the depths of cyberspace.

So start off with the journalist's friend, that clean sheet of white paper, and some basic terms of reference.

Consider and organize your potential content

'As the Internet provides us all with the freedom to publish information, it quietly burdens us with the responsibility to organize that information.' Rosenfeld and Morville (1998)

The next stage is to think carefully about your content, but in a way that may not come naturally to you. Think not just of the individual stories or the tone of your journalism, but how you will arrange it into groups and what will be the structure between those groups.

This approach may bother you, because it makes you feel more like a librarian than a journalist. But you must get used to it because the distinction is not valid in the online world. The web environment can be hugely liberating for the user, but only if there has been careful planning by the provider. It is an apparent paradox, but without structure, there is no freedom. It will also make your job much easier and more enjoyable in the long run.

The first thing to put on your sheet of paper is an outline of the potential content for your site. This should not be item by item, rather some broad headings, including features (e.g. daily news) and functions (e.g. help page). If you want to feel important, you can tell yourself you are compiling an outline content inventory.

At this stage, a list will suffice, but Rosenfeld and Morville recommend that a hierarchical model, like a family tree, is another useful starting point:

The top-down approach allows you to quickly get a handle on the scope of the web site without going through an extensive content inventory process. You can begin identifying the major content areas and exploring possible organization schemes that will provide access to the content.

A hierarchy can be your starting point, but it does not have to be your end point. Most web sites are based on hierarchies but, as we will see, there are alternative site structures.

Next, you should start to put your content into groups/ categories/sections. This is where a lot of sites go wrong and can be your first point of departure with your users, even before you have actually gathered any material or filled a single page. You *must* put yourself in your users' shoes and ask the following questions.

- What will interest the users most? If this sounds familiar, it is. It is the essential canon that informed and guided our news gathering and writing in earlier chapters. This is why content organization can be a seamless extension of your journalism. This may sound obvious, but some sites do not appear to give it much thought, perhaps because they do not give the content providers enough say in designing their information architecture.
- How will the users want/expect this information to be grouped/ arranged? This is perhaps the most difficult area. Corporate sites in particular can suffer from assuming too much user knowledge of their organization. The providers of the information who spend each working day immersed in the structural intricacies of their organizations, find it very difficult to distance themselves, to put themselves on the outside looking in. User testing here is essential at the prototype stage.
- What are the tasks the users will want to perform? Will they know exactly what they are looking for or will they want to browse? Do they want summaries or print-offs?

Understanding if your user is likely to know what they're looking for is a major consideration when organizing your content. With this knowledge, you can employ another method of categorization, described by Rosenfeld and Morville as 'organization schemes'. They identify two kinds:

- exact, for example alphabetical, chronological and geographical – these suit users who know exactly what they are looking for and what it will be called, but are less helpful for those who do not; and
- ambiguous, this is by topic (e.g. the phone book yellow pages), by task (e.g. booking different types of holiday) or by user group (where you have two or more distinct user groups with different requirements, you can group the content to suit them).

As Rosenfeld and Morville acknowledge, ambiguous organization schemes are the most difficult but can be the most useful, particularly for those users who do not know exactly what they are looking for:

In an ambiguous organization scheme, someone other than the user has made an intellectual decision to group items together. This grouping of related items supports an associative learning process that may enable the user to make new connections and reach better conclusions. While ambiguous organization schemes require more work and introduce a messy element of subjectivity, they often prove more valuable to their user than exact schemes.

You should also remember that your users are not a static entity. If they like what they see, they will come back. Yet, when they return, they will be different users, more knowledgeable because of their initial visit. So you have to consider grouping information and providing levels of access that will satisfy the changing knowledge and needs of the users.

As David Siegel (1997) puts it:

Information designers talk about granularity – putting just the right amount of information in front of the user at any one time. The more expert the people become, the more an information space should adapt to give them the power tools they need.

Putting the content sections into a structure

By now, you are beginning to formulate the basic structure to your site. You may not have followed Rosenfeld and Morville's suggestion about roughing out your content with a basic hierarchy, but you will still find yourself drawing boxes connected by lines, indicating how they relate to each other. Each line will represent a link from one page/area to another. Your list is turning into a flow diagram.

Next, a good tip from Robin Williams and John Tollett (2000). As your ideas come together, they are bound to change. So rather than sitting knee-deep in crumpled balls of paper, grab the pad of sticky-backed reminder notes and devote each one to a separate area of content. Then get a large sheet of white paper, or even a whiteboard, and move the stickies around to try out different structures and relationships between content. At this stage, each stickie might represent a separate content area or sub-area, but as your ideas mature (and if your board is big enough), each could come to represent an individual web page.

So you are now surrounded by sticky notes and a more detailed flow diagram is emerging. What shape should it be? As we have noted, the instinct is to place categories and pages in a hierarchy, like a family tree, with your home page at the top. That is one of the most common web site structures, but it is not the only one.

Lynch and Horton (1999) give a breakdown of the four different types of site structures.

1 The sequence – this places pages in a line with the only link available supporting the linear path from A to B to C. This sounds like a contradiction of the medium with its non-linear consumption pattern. However, it is a useful method for

presenting training information, particularly where it could be confusing or even dangerous if someone skipped a section.

2 The grid – this can be useful where you have a lot of information within a particular field that shares common characteristics. For example, if you were building a site about the English Football Premiership, you might want to list each club and then look at each club's facilities, player signings, disciplinary record, etc. With a grid system, your user could follow each club through all the club's pages; or they could cut across the clubs and examine by category (e.g. look at pages listing the disciplinary record of each club). You can organize the content of grid-structured sites with a database. Indeed, databases can be used for any part of your site where you would put large amounts of searchable information of a similar nature and composition, such as a catalogue or staff directory. However, as Rosenfeld and Morville point out, they can be very expensive and time consuming to construct and will need the input of a programmer. Do not undertake them lightly.

3 The hierarchy – as already noted, this is a common structure for web sites. Lynch and Horton believe it is 'the best way to organize most complex bodies of information ... Hierarchical diagrams are very familiar in corporate and institutional life, so most users find this structure easy to understand. A hierarchical organization also imposes a useful discipline on your own analytical approach to your content, because hierarchies are practical only with well-organized material.' The depth or flatness of your hierarchy is another issue. If you have a very flat structure, with one home page leading to a single secondary level with multiple pages, the menu on your home page will be extensive, some might say unwieldy and discouraging. If, instead, you opt for a very deep structure, with different levels of menu and sub-menus before you arrive at the content, you risk alienating the user, who may have to click through too many pages of what are called 'nested menus' to get to what he or she wants. As ever, it is a matter of balance. Interviewed since writing his book, Louis Rosenfeld says that user preference is moving towards the flat

structure: 'The growing consensus is that users want the "broad and shallow". People don't trust that, if the site makes choices for them on the main page, those would be the ones they would go by if they were clicking through. We're finding, rather surprisingly, that they would rather a front page of 100 links.' And a search engine.

4 The web – this sounds like the structure most suited to the online medium, as users are allowed to 'follow their interests in a unique, heuristic, idiosyncratic pattern'. However, although this pursuit of the 'free flow of ideas' is fine as a model for user consumption patterns, using it as a structure for your site is another matter altogether. As Rosenfeld and Morville point out, this hypertext structural model can be employed at the level of the story or information chunk, but even then, only with care and within a more organized primary site structure, such as a hierarchy. Let the users spin their own intricate web of page visits but within your clear structure, just like the spider which needs to attach its creation to *something* solid.

It is possible for a site to have two organizational structures within it. You could start off with a hierarchy that could flow into a part of your site that is, for example, a sequence. A hospital web site could have a hierarchical structure for the home page with different sections flowing from it, but if one of those sections was for young patients, a sequential structure might be the best way to show what happens when they come to hospital for an examination – a good use of the web to introduce the idea to this user group in the re-assuring environment of their home.

The important things to remember are:

■ have a structure/s that is/are appropriate to your content and user;
■ do not offer too much variation within one site; and
■ signpost any changes clearly and offer clear navigation around each structure.

But wait a minute, I hear a jeep approaching.

David Siegel tends not to talk much about hierarchies and grids. Hierarchies were the preserve of what he calls the 'second generation' sites. By 1997, he had moved onto the third generation. These sites, according to Siegel, 'give visitors a complete experience'. They should 'pull visitors through by tantalizing them with something exciting on every page'. They have front doors, entry tunnels (a short sequence of pages to lead or tempt you into a site), a core site area with pages fanning out from it and a defined exit point or tunnel so you can see your visitors off the virtual premises as any good host would, with a parting gift such as a prize draw entry.

This is a completely different way of visualizing the user experience – more guided and more linear. It is striking that Siegel frequently uses metaphor to describe his approach. He compares visiting a site to going to a restaurant – a very 'real world' experience. He emphasizes the virtual element of online as much as the ability to deliver large and variable volumes of information to a range of different users. Yet you can be absolutely certain that David Siegel's sites are carefully structured and such structures should not be excluded from your thinking when developing your site. Be open to all influences. Go and visit one of his 'restaurants'. You may get a taste for the cuisine.

The important thing is to have a structure, however you modify any of the above models. Too many web sites mushroom without form or shape. Therein lies disaster.[6]

Once you have grouped all your content and chosen a structure, you are still only part way through the design process. You may think that it is too early to be thinking about production, but remember this is a concurrent, not consecutive process. So while you are scrutinizing your content, you may as well also categorize it by type. This will help you devise your implementation programme, as certain types of content will provide a bed-rock and may be less time-consuming and costly to produce. This is the content you may wish to build first, when you get round to it.

---

[6] Structure – shallow or deep, web or hierarchy – is not the whole picture. Steve Krug (2000) feels that what really counts is 'not the number of clicks it takes to get me to what I want (although there are limits) but rather how hard each click is – the amount of thought required, and the amount of uncertainty about whether I am making the right choice.' Satisfying that demand will depend on a number of other factors other than structure.

The four main types of content are:

- static – any information that is unlikely to change, for example contact details, site rules and codes of conduct;
- dynamic – 'what's new' sections, daily news and articles; links and references;
- functional – menus, navigation bars, etc.; and
- interactive – e-mail, members' areas, forms and scripts.

Eventually, your site structure will mature into a site map. At this level of detail, it will be possible to spot content areas that will be overloaded. These could be further sub-divided. It may also show that your chosen structure is struggling to deliver your content needs.

This is a good time to return to your mission statement and check you have not lost sight of your goals. It is also time for a reality check. Look again at your resources and ask yourself if you really can build this site and, most importantly, run it. If the answer is 'Yes', move on to the next phase.

Page inventories

Now that you have a mission, content inventory, content group-ings and site structure and map, it is time to start thinking about what is going to appear on your web pages.

Note that this is not the same as thinking about what your pages will finally look like. It is too early for that. Considering what will be on each of your pages will, of course, influence the way it looks. However, the reverse of this process is another matter entirely and not recommended for news or information pages.

So let's consider what is going to be on each page. You compiled a story inventory when separating your information into chunks, and a content inventory when structuring your site. Now you can also try a page inventory.

So far, you broadly know the categories of information that will appear in each page and you may even have some sample content. If you were writing a book, that would be enough, and once the content was finalized, you could move on to the design. However, the web makes the process a little more complicated. The freedom enjoyed by users roaming where they wish, gathering content, comes at a price that you, the provider, have to pay.

So, in addition to content, your page inventory should include information:

- telling your users where they are within the web and the site, and to help them find their way around all the other pages; and
- helping the users to operate in a screen-based, interactive environment.

We've looked at content. Let's see what's required for these other two. Then we can start putting it all together.

Give users the tools to find their way around the sections

This is where the boundaries within the traditional nomenclature really start to blur. Where does the navigation end and the interface begin? So let's put these terms to one side and look at the essential requirements. Let's be 'bottom up'. What must you offer on your page?

The first thing you must offer is consistency. You may want to offer a rich mix and variety of content, but if you want users to find it you must give them clear and consistent guidance around your site structure. Remember, not all your visitors will come through the front door. Some may be delivered to a single page, deep within your site, by a link from elsewhere. So each page should be able to stand alone editorially with a clear identity and provenance.

Each of your pages should:

- contain your site identity, usually a consistent logo or heading;
- state who created the content on it;
- say when it was created or revised;
- provide an informative title for the content;
- indicate which area of the site the user is currently in;
- provide a link to the home page;

- provide a link to an index or site map;
- provide a search facility;
- provide a way for the users to return to previous pages;
- provide a linkable summary of where else on the site they can go; and
- link them to web content anywhere that is specifically related to that page.

Not much really to fit on to the 'real estate' of your single web page, is it? And, of course, you have got your content too.

There are certain standard features that can support navigation, such as links being underlined and the cursor arrow turning into a hand when over an interactive area. In theory, your browser window can help with backtracking by offering 'Forward', 'Back' and 'History' buttons, although these do not help users who have parachuted in from another site to navigate yours. The 'Back' button will only return them to the previous site they were visiting. So you've still got a bit to do.

Little surprise then, that designers can get it wrong. Some of the common mistakes are:

- forgetting some of these key elements;
- not applying them consistently;
- not displaying them clearly (e.g. putting search facilities at the bottom of the page and, so, usually off-screen unless the user scrolls);
- allowing these features to take over the page, squeezing out the content;
- putting ambiguous labels on content categories;
- putting labels on content categories that require the knowledge the user is seeking in the first place to be understood;
- subjugating the purpose of the navigation to the 'look' of the site; and
- use of inappropriate metaphor.

Metaphor is a tricky area. Get it right and it can simplify your navigation and improve your user interface. Get it wrong and it can dominate your site and contort your content organization.

Metaphor is when you use an object or scenario that people are familiar with as a vessel for your site construction and a vehicle for navigation. Car dashboards, TV remote controls, houses and the human body have all been used as metaphors.

Metaphors can put your content together in a way that your user can instantly relate to, but as David Siegel explains (1997), they must be well designed:

> Metaphors are vehicles of exploration. Make it simple, consistent and easy to get around. A good metaphor puts the light switch where you expect to find it. A bad metaphor makes you learn a whole new set of commands to enter. Well-executed metaphors make it difficult to get lost.

Metaphors must be not only well designed, but also well conceived. The problem with metaphors is they are usually applied literally. A site for a car parts company is going to use a metaphor linked to the automobile, not the human body or an art gallery. However, the use of metaphor and the kind of metaphor should be driven by the range of content and the structure of the site, not just some literal association with the subject-matter. Users will relate to the metaphor in the same way they would relate to its real-life equivalent. That is its whole purpose. An exploratory metaphor (human body, gallery, etc.) may actually suit the content of the car parts site better than the static metaphor of the car dashboard. But, of course, this would also be unsuitable as its literal association would seem out of place. Who gives to an art gallery to buy a car part? It's difficult to get the right combination of suitable literal association and appropriate framework for content and navigation. Metaphors – handle with care.

So let's get back to our essentials. The 'linkable summary of where else on the site they can go' will point users to various utilities such as 'Help' or 'Checkout' for e-commerce sites. It will also list your content categories, decided at the structuring stage. This is all part of the 'persistent' navigation that is found on every page.

You can also offer 'local' navigation, specific to individual pages. This shows what is on offer, not across the site, but at the level your user is currently at. Steve Krug (2000) believes a common failing of web design is not giving the same amount of attention to this lower level navigation as is devoted to the top end:

> In so many sites, as soon as you get past the second level, the navigation breaks down and becomes ad hoc ... But the reality is that users usually spend as much time on lower level pages as they do at the top. And unless you have worked out top-to-bottom navigation from the beginning, it's very hard to graft it on later and come up with something consistent. ... The moral? It's vital (when designing) to have sample pages that show the navigation for all the potential levels of the site before you start arguing about the colour scheme for the home page.

Another useful navigation tool is the use of 'breadcrumbs'. Taking their lead from the fairytale characters Hansel and Gretel, some designers will display the user's journey through various levels of the hierarchical structure as a series of headings connected with arrows, usually at the top of the page. This works particularly well on sites with deep structures, providing instant location for the user who can also click on any heading to jump back to a previous level.

This all helps people to find their way around the site. But keep stepping back from your page plan. Are you building up too much 'noise' or visual clutter? Don't forget – the content should be the centre of attention.

When you find yourself talking like this, it is time to get serious about layout and other elements of graphic design. But all the time keep whispering to yourself 'interface, interface, interface'.

Present the whole package effectively

Page layout and design

What some people start with, we have left until the end. You will have thought a lot about page layout and design before now, but the mental activity should have been at three in the morning, over breakfast or in the shower. It will have been tugging at your sleeve for attention, but should not have been the focus of your thoughts. If you don't adopt this discipline, you might find yourself being told that you cannot present the content structure or the navigation the way you want because 'there isn't room in the design'.

Similarly, you will have favourite fonts and colours, but you need the ones that complement the layout and reinforce the overall design requirement to communicate your content most effectively to your users.

What follows puts the emphasis on graphic design because this is the point of sale, so to speak. You have to get the users' attention when they first arrive on your site. If they feel comfortable with/stimulated by the look and feel of the first page they see AND if the content is appropriate and well organized, they are more likely to progress to the next page. With each new page visited, the content takes greater responsibility for holding the reader's interest. However, the graphical element must remain as a reinforcer, a source of continuity and navigational aide.

That is quite a stretch – from siren voice to trusted guide – which is why graphic design is such a demanding area. Although the scope of this book is broad, a detailed breakdown of the implementation of graphic design is beyond it. It is better to focus on some basic principles. If you are 'doing a site' for your company, these guidelines may lead you away from the deepest elephant traps. If you are part of a web development team, they may give you a voice around the table in this most critical of areas.

Robin Williams and John Tollett (2000) identify the following four key principles when designing your page.

- Alignment – it is possible to place elements such as text on the left-hand side, the right-hand side or in the middle. Choose one of these alignments and stick to it. Do not mix them, as it disorientates the reader. Centred alignments should be used with care. Centring text tends to weaken the visual line as the edges have no definition.
- Proximity – if items on a page are close together, it suggests to the reader that these items are related. Ensure that items that should be related (e.g. picture and caption) are placed in closer proximity than those that should not. Squint your eyes and see

how items are related spatially. If the result is misleading, adjust the proximities.

- Repetition – consistent use of layout, colour, typography, navigation buttons, etc. throughout a site will 'ground' it and help users to orientate themselves around it.
- Contrast – this is required to pull readers into a page and guide them through it. Contrasting type, colour, graphics, etc. will provide a focal point and a visual hierarchy.

Lynch and Horton describe graphic design as 'visual information management'. Establishing a visual hierarchy will contribute to this, emphasizing and, therefore, prioritizing information through, for example, different sizes of type.

A page must also have visual balance. This can be symmetrical, asymmetrical or radial. People usually find symmetrical balance more appealing. This is why beginners often centre text, because it pleases their eye, despite the problems it causes.

Heavy lines, large pictures and blocks of text all contribute to the balance or imbalance of a page as well as the hierarchy. The size of one element on a page in relation to the others is also a factor.

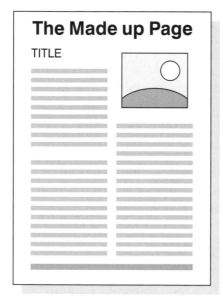
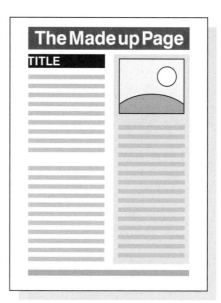

Figure 7.5: When designing your page layout, consider the use of contrast for effect.

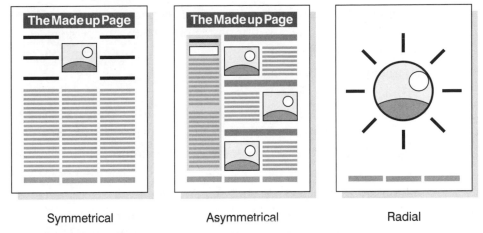

Figure 7.6: The page must have visual balance, whether symmetrical, asymmetrical or radial.

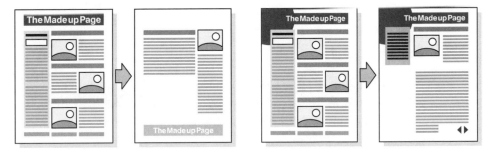

Figure 7.7: Repetition can provide a visual structure to your page.

Do not forget the white space

I often think Count Basie would have made a great graphic designer. Maybe he was, away from the day job. Basie knew how to play the notes well enough. But he was a master of the spaces in between.

So it is with the use of white space. As David Siegel (1997) notes:

> White space – the space between visual elements – is an integral part of the message ... the white space tells you where one section ends and the other begins ... systematic use of white space can vastly improve the presentation of text for easier reading and better comprehension.

Designers have always been aware of its potency on the printed page. The screen is no different. Some of the most successful web pages use the background to the content to form a design as much as the content itself.

But be careful. The use of alignment in text and the square edges of the images add visual guides to a page. They can imply a grid system which can enhance white space, but also trap it. These areas of trapped space can interrupt the flow of the page, affecting the balance of individual elements and ultimately the balance of your whole page.

The successful use of white space is a great skill. At this stage, it is best to be aware of its potency. It is not just the receptacle of the text, images, etc. It has a visual weight of its own.

Use of colour

For some, white space is a non-issue because they flood their screens with fuchsia, turquoise or lime green. Each to his own. Colour is a powerful tool in the designer's box, so you are advised to use it carefully.

Colour can say much about your site and you. It should be used in line with your mission statement. Sounds absurd, doesn't it. Colour designed by mission. But if the purpose of your design is to communicate, colour is an important part of this process.

The truth is that, on many web sites, colour has a far greater potential to disrupt, annoy and repel users than to attract them. The wrong use of a coloured text on a differently coloured background can render Pulitzer prize winning journalism unreadable. Colours that extend beyond the pallette of web browsers will result in a look which was not what the designer intended. Harsh, bright or overpowering colours can make screen reading too arduous.

If you think carefully about your users and what they want, you can provide a colour scheme that will enhance your message and encourage user involvement.

Different types of colour

There are four different classifications of colour. Knowing them and how they relate to each other will guide you towards wise colour choice.

■ Primary – red, blue and green (not yellow). The difference to the paintbox primaries is because, in web design, the primary colours are defined by how a monitor works. Do not combine these colours on screen (e.g. red text on a blue background).
■ Secondary – the colours created by mixing two of the primary colours.
■ Analogous – the colours that are next to each other on the colour wheel. They are closely related because they have a colour in common (e.g. green, yellow-green and yellow). So analogous colours are usually harmonious and pleasing to the eye.
■ Complementary – these colours are opposite each other on the colour wheel. They can look dynamic and exciting and almost seem to vibrate when placed side by side. Be warned, however, as they can actually fuzz detail, especially text.

Type

As David Siegel (1997) notes:

> Type plays an important role on almost any web page . . . Compared to other kinds of graphics, type is an inexpensive source of raw material that can be used over and over to great effect. You don't have to hire an illustrator, take photographs or create custom illustrations. Simply use type to give your pages a unique look and feel.

You will be familiar with the font facility on your word processing package. Choose a certain type and size and it appears on the screen. However, it is not as simple as that on the web. You may use a certain font on your site, but your user may have selected a different font as the default on his or her browser. You can override this with the design specifications of your page but, as

Oldstyle
Modern
Sans Serif
Script
DECORATIVE

Figure 7.8: Fonts come in different groups.

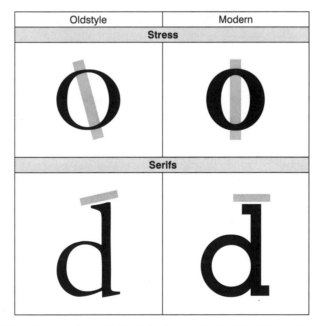

	Oldstyle	Modern
Stress		

Serifs

Figure 7.9: The choice of font is important. An 'oldstyle' typeface, with its slanted stresses and serifs, can be easier to read in large quantities of body text than a more upright, modern font, particularly those fonts which are also without (sans) serif. These can work well for headings.

Williams and Tollett (2000) advise, it is dangerous to overdo this:

> Accept the limitations of the World Wide Web and let go of total control. Don't create designs that are dependent on text being a certain font, size or in a certain place. Don't tell the visitor how to set their defaults – maybe they like their defaults the way they are. It's not their problem to make their system match your ideal – it's your problem to work around the variables.

Williams and Tollett believe the two main issues for type are readability and legibility.

- Readability is important when reading a lot of body text. A serif text such as Times New Roman or Georgia is often used because the extra lines on the edge of each character helps the flow of our eye movement and makes it less tiring to read large amounts of the text. However, poor screen resolution can reduce the benefit of this by making the serifs less distinct.
- Legibility is important for short sections of text such as headlines. Sans serif fonts such as Arial or Verdana, are preferable, not just for headlines but also the body text if the serif font is indistinct.

Another issue to consider about type is the use of capital and lowercase letters. Lynch and Horton (1999) point out that 'we read primarily by recognizing the overall shape of words, not by parsing each letter and then assembling a recognizable word'. Words spelt out in capitals offer few clue shapes and so are hard work when you have to read a lot of them. Also, if you want to use capitals to emphasize something, you lose that power of emphasis if everything is in uppercase.

Line length is another important consideration. Lynch and Horton (1999) remind us that:

> At normal reading distance, the eye's span of acute focus is only about three inches wide ... wider lines of text require

readers to move their heads slightly or strain their eye muscles to track over the long lines of text.

So avoid edge-to-edge lines of text. It is the reason why newspapers and magazines have always used column widths. Although it is more difficult to do on the web, the widespread use of tables now gives designers more control over line length and, therefore, readability.

Now you have all the main ingredients to lay your page out. So what are you going to opt for, something unique and groundbreaking or tried and tested? The warring natives, as ever are not helpful. 'Try splash screens,' says one. 'Splash screens must die,' says another. Terrific.

Once again, you need to go back to your journalistic roots. There is a magpie in every journalist, constantly seeking shiny nuggets of information to hoard away for a rainy day. It is the same with web design. Just as journalists are urged to read, read and read, you should surf, surf and surf, looking for design ideas. When you do, you will find that there are surprisingly few fundamentally new ones. As Jakob Nielsen says, if 90% of web sites are doing it, maybe you should too. At least to get you going.

Common web layouts

The two most common examples of web layout are the L (or inverted L) and the I (or sometimes a T).

The L and inverted L layout is used a lot on sites such as news sites, which require a large amount of navigation upfront to enable the user to see what is available. It uses asymmetrical balance as the main construct of the page.

The I and the T layout works well on a site that has a lot of, but a limited range of, content. If your site does not have such a specific focus and offers a wider range of services, try placing the main content down the middle of the screen with extra navigation at each side, making a T shape. The navigation on the left is usually reserved for navigation within a site and that on the right for navigation within a section or story.

If a page requires scrolling, the navigation is often repeated, providing the I pattern.

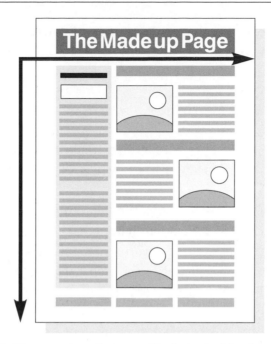

Figure 7.10: Many news sites use the inverted L shape layout.

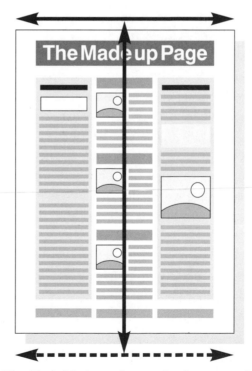

Figure 7.11: The T and I shape layout is the second standard form of page layout.

**Ensure the whole package works within the online environ-
ment and seeing what your users think before going live.**

Interface and usability

You must ensure that the whole package works within the
online environment – see what your users think before going
live.

You may have settled on your chosen layout and filled it with
content and navigation, but you still have some work to do. You
need to be sure that it works, particularly within the interactive on-
screen environment of the web. Steve Krug defines usability as
making sure 'that a person of average (or even below average)
ability and experience can use the thing – whether it's a web site,
a fighter jet or a revolving door – for its intended purpose without
getting hopelessly frustrated'.

Krug's first law of usability, indeed it is the title of his book on
the subject, is 'Don't make me think.' He believes that a web site
should be self-evident (i.e. it should be immediately obvious what
it is and how to use it) or at least self-explanatory (i.e. just
requiring a little thought to work it out). This is because users
scan web pages, choose the first reasonable option they see and
usually muddle through rather than working out just how the site
works. Faced with this, 'if web pages are going to be effective,
they have to work most of their magic at a glance'.

Krug believes that anything that makes people think adds to
their 'cognitive workload' and increases the 'mental chatter'. The
sort of things that make users think include:

- ambiguous names for sections or functions;
- links and buttons that are not obviously clickable;
- confusing options for utilities such as search engines; and
- poor navigation.

The answer is to consider these and other issues from the outset
but also to user test your site. Designers lose perspective. Users
give it back.

Krug may be a usability expert, but he thinks and writes like a journalist, informing the reader with clarity, purpose and wit. The web sites that follow his advice may hope to do the same. Interface design and usability engineering may seem far removed from the world of news value and delivery, but on the World Wide Web, they live on the same block.

Further reading and references

Algie, B. (1997). *How to Activate your Web Site*. Que Pub.

Brand, S. (1994). *How Buildings Learn*. Penguin.

Brown, J. and Duguid, P. (2000). *The Social Life of Information*. Harvard Business School.

Burdman, J. (1999). *Collaborative Web Development*. Addison-Wesley.

Davis, J. and Merritt, S. (1998). *Web Design Wow Book*. Peach Pit Press.

Feldman, T. (1997). *Introduction to Digital Media*. Routledge.

Fleming, J. (1998). *Web Navigation: Designing the User Experience*. O'Reilly.

Garcia, M.R. (1997). *Redesigning Print for the Web*. Hayden.

Haggard, M. (1998). *Survival Guide to Web Site Development*. Microsoft Press.

Haig, M. (2000). *E-PR*. Kogan Page.

Krug, S. (2000). *Don't Make Me Think*. Circle.

Lynch, P.J. and Horton, S. (1999). *Web Style Guide*. Yale.

Negroponte, N. (1995). *Being Digital*. Coronet.

Niederst, J. (1999). *Web Design in a Nutshell*. O'Reilly.

Nielsen, J. (1999). *Designing Web Usability*. New Riders.

Norman, D.A. (1988). *The Design of Everyday Things*. Basic Books.

Rosenfeld, L. and Morville, P. (1998). *Information Architecture*. O'Neill.

Siegel, D. (1997). *Creating Killer Web Sites*. 2nd edition. Hayden.

Veen, J. (1997). *Hot Wired Style*. Wired Books.

Weiss, A. (1997). *Web Authoring Desk Reference*. Hayden.

Williams, R. and Tollett, J. (2000). *The Non-Designers Design Book*. 2nd edition. Peach Pit Press.

- www.best.com/~jthom/usability/toc/htm – usability testing tools and other resources.
- www.bluewave.com and www.razorfish.com – two examples of international web design houses.
- www.cnet.com – a major computing and technology site, including a useful section on web page building.
- www.hotwired.lycos.com/webmonkey – Wired's invaluable web developer's resource.
- www.lynda.com – the web site of leading Dreamweaver exponent Lynda Weinmann.
- http://patricklynch.net – a valuable resource from one of the authors of the *Web Style Guide*.
- www.theobvious.com – a great URL for Michael Sippey's stimulating site, commenting on Internet technology, business and culture. The site design is a model of restraint.
- www.useit.com – Jakob Nielsen's influential site and the place where it all started.
- www.webpagesthatsuck.com – learn how to do it by seeing how not to do.

Index

 **Focal Press**

www.focalpress.com

Join Focal Press on-line

As a member you will enjoy the following benefits:

- an email bulletin with **information on new books**
- a regular **Focal Press Newsletter**:
  - o featuring a selection of new titles
  - o keeps you informed of **special offers, discounts and freebies**
  - o alerts you to **Focal Press news and events** such as author signings and seminars
- complete access to **free content** and reference material on the focalpress site, such as the focalXtra articles and commentary from our authors
- a **Sneak Preview** of selected titles (sample chapters) *before* they publish
- a chance to have your say on our **discussion boards** and **review books** for other Focal readers

Focal Club Members are invited to give us feedback on our products and services.
Email: worldmarketing@focalpress.com – we want to hear your views!

Membership is **FREE**. To join, visit our website and register. If you require any further information regarding the on-line club please contact:

> Emma Hales, Marketing Manager
> Email: emma.hales@repp.co.uk
> Tel: +44 (0) 1865 314556
> Fax: +44 (0)1865 314572
> Address: Focal Press, Linacre House,
> Jordan Hill, Oxford, UK, OX2 8DP

Catalogue

For information on all Focal Press titles, our full catalogue is available online at www.focalpress.com and all titles can be purchased here via secure online ordering, or contact us for a free printed version:

USA
Email: christine.degon@bhusa.com
Tel: +1 781 904 2607

Europe and rest of world
Email: jo.coleman@repp.co.uk
Tel: +44 (0)1865 314220

Potential authors

If you have an idea for a book, please get in touch:

USA
editors@focalpress.com

Europe and rest of world
focal.press@repp.co.uk